The famous German artist Albrecht Dürer met and sketched a party of Irish soldiers in 1521

Nothing but the same old story

I was just about nineteen
When I landed on their shore
With my eyes big as headlights
Like the thousands and thousands who came before.
I was going to be something...
Smiled at the man scrutinising my face,
As I stepped down off the gangway.

Came down to their city
Where I worked for many's a year.
Built a hundred houses
Must've pulled half a million pints of beer
Livin' under suspicion.
Puttin' up with the hatred and fear in their eyes
You can see that you are nothin' but a murderer
In their eyes, we're nothin' but a bunch of murderers.

I'm sick of watching them break up
Every time some bird brain puts us down.
Makin' jokes on the radio...
Guess it helps them all drown out the sound
Of crumbling foundations.
Any fool can see the writing on the wall
But they just don't believe that its happening.

There's a crowd say I'm alright...
Say they like my turn of phrase
Take me round to their parties
Like some dressed up monkey in a cage.
And I play my accordion
Oh! But when the wine seeps through the facade.
Its nothing but the same old story
Nothing but the same old story.

<u>Paul Brady</u> from 'Hard Station'

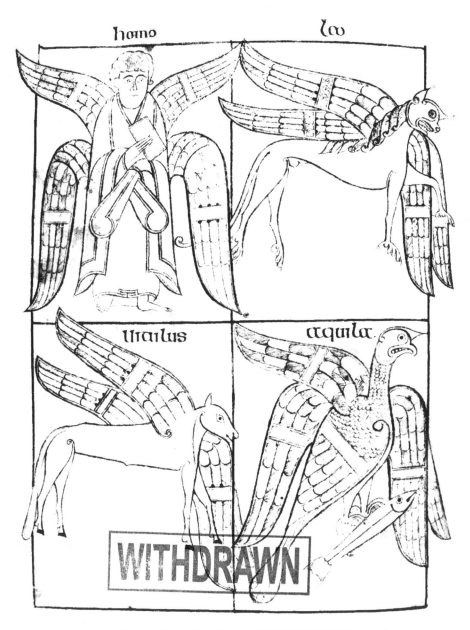

homo   leo

uitulus   aquila

Above: A page from the Book of Armagh, written in the early ninth century

Left: A gravestone from Clonmacnoise, Co. Offaly

First published in 1984 by Information on Ireland,
London. 2nd and 3rd impressions 1985.
4th 1986. 5th 1988. 6th 1991.

Published in 1996 by Sásta,
The Ashton Centre, 5 Churchill Street, Belfast BT15 2BP.
Reprinted 1998.

Text by Liz Curtis.
Produced by Gill Biggs, Dagmar Coward, Oliver Donohue,
John Lloyd, Alastair Renwick.
With thanks for their help to Peter Berresford Ellis, Steve
Brennan, Flann Campbell, Mary Campbell, Seamus Carey,
Mary Hickman, Michael Maguire, Brian Parsons, Duncan
Smith, Irish Video Project.

Picture research by Alastair Renwick.
Designed by Adrian Yeeles/Artworkers.
Typeset by Lithosphere Printing Co-operative Ltd.
Printed by the Russell Press Ltd., Radford Mill, Norton
Street, Nottingham NG7 3HJ, tel. 0115 978 4505.

Extract from 'Hard Station' reproduced by kind permission
of Paul Brady and Rondor Music (London) Ltd.

ISBN 1 901005 00 3

Trade distribution by Turnaround Distribution,
Unit 3, Olympia Trading Estate, Coburg Road,
London N22 6TZ, tel. 0181 829 3000,
fax 0181 881 5088.

The racism and the conditions that the Irish community face today are deeply rooted in British colonial history. Although it has varied in degree, anti-Irish sentiment is directly linked to Irish resistance to English rule in Ireland.

The needs of the Irish community, one in six of London's population, cannot be ignored any further by the GLC or other institutions committed to racial harmony.

I welcome this book and feel it will play a valuable part in helping to remove the negative and racist stereotyping which so often adversely affects the Irish community in Britain.

Ken Livingstone

KEN LIVINGSTONE

IRISH BULLS

'There is a subject which dilates the heart of every true Briton, which relaxes his muscles, however rigid, to a smile, which opens his lips, however closed, to conversation... For who can forbear to laugh at the bare idea of an Irish bull?'

That passage was written by the Anglo-Irish novelist Maria Edgeworth and her father, Richard Lovell Edgeworth, in a book that was first published in 1802.[1] The book was a sharp and witty attack on 'Irish bulls', which we today call 'Irish jokes'.

Anti-Irish prejudice, from which anti-Irish humour springs, is a very old theme in English culture. It is one of the oldest manifestations of the pervasive delusion that the English are a culturally and physically uniform people – white, Anglo-Saxon and Protestant – who are 'superior' to every other kind of person.

The renewal of conflict in the North of Ireland in 1969 brought with it an upsurge in anti-Irish prejudice in England. Politicians and media commentators have refused to recognise Britain's responsibility for the 'troubles', and instead have portrayed Britain as a disinterested third party, and the Irish as irrational and innately prone to violence. Newspaper cartoonists have taken up the theme, depicting the Irish as bestial or sub-human, while anti-Irish jokes have spread the message that the Irish are 'stupid'.

This theme has been promoted by television comedians, by the sale of 'Irish' novelty goods such as mugs with their handles inside, and by countless 'Irish joke' books. Indeed, this type of humour is so pervasive that the very word 'Irish' is enough to provoke roars of laughter from television studio audiences, and is used in everyday conversation to describe behaviour that is confusing or illogical.

Such images of the Irish, far from being 'harmless', have had a real and adverse effect on the thinking of English people. A survey published in 1984 of nearly 800 children at a Nottingham comprehensive school revealed that of seven groups – English, German, Indian, Irish, Jewish, Pakistani and West Indian – the Irish were the least liked, followed closely by the Pakistanis. For the purposes of the survey, the children themselves were divided into four groups: White British, West Indian, Pakistani and Indian. The Irish were seen as 'violent' and 'dull', and only a minority of the children – all in the 'White British' category, which included children of Irish descent – attributed a positive characteristic – 'cheerful' – to the Irish.[2]

The widespread association of the Irish with stupidity has for years caused concern, anger and distress in Britain's several million strong Irish community. Some have been tempted to deny their Irish identity. For example, a schoolteacher told a researcher that, 'In the school, there is a feeling that anything to do with Ireland is backward or stupid, and the Irish children would be ashamed of wearing the shamrock.' A child said, 'Some Irish people come to England to live and some people take the mickey out of them when they speak, so they try to get the accent out.'[3] The term 'to take the mickey' – 'Mickey', like 'Paddy', is an old term for an Irish person – testifies to the degree to which the view of the Irish as objects of derision is ingrained.

Many Irish people, however, have recognised that anti-Irish prejudice, now as in the past, says nothing about their own level of intelligence, but is rather a symptom of English ignorance and self-deception – not only about Ireland and Irish people, but about England's history and the British government's role in Ireland today.

A panel from the Book of Durrow, written in the mid-seventh century

THE NORMANS

The English notion that the Irish are inferior to themselves has its roots way back in the twelfth century, when Norman feudal lords invaded Ireland. Like all dominant groups – whether peoples, classes or races, or the male sex in cultures which oppress women – the Normans not only physically subjugated and exploited their victims but also devalued them.

In the twelfth century, neither England nor Ireland were 'nations' in the modern sense. In England and Wales, the Normans were a French-speaking aristocracy whose rule still extended to Normandy across the Channel. They had conquered England a hundred years earlier, laying waste the northern regions in the process, and had reduced the Anglo-Saxon farmers to serfdom. The condition of serfs was described by Pope Innocent III:

> The serf serves; he is terrified with threats, wearied by corvées [forced services], afflicted with blows, despoiled for his possessions… O extreme condition of bondage! Nature brought freemen to birth but fortune hath made bondmen. The serf must needs suffer, and no man is suffered to feel for him, he is compelled to mourn, and no man is permitted to mourn with him. He is not his own man, but no man is his![4]

The Normans did not have a high opinion of the native English. The churchman and writer Gerald of Wales wrote that the English were 'the most worthless of all peoples under heaven… In their own lands the English are slaves to the Normans, the most abject slaves.'[5]

Illustration from the Book of Durrow

In the last half of the twelfth century, Norman lords, soon followed by King Henry II, sought to increase their wealth and power by conquering territory in Ireland.

Ireland was not then organised on the feudal model. It was inhabited by a loose federation of Celtic peoples – cousins of the Britons whom the Anglo-Saxons had displaced from England – whose social organisation was, compared with the feudal system, relatively egalitarian. Although there were distinct social classes – warriors, priests and lawyers, farmers of various grades – land was held in common, kings were elected, and women had a relatively high status. The society was regulated through an elaborate system of laws, known as the Brehon laws, which made kinship groups responsible for the actions of their members and which were concerned more with resolving disputes than with inflicting punishment.

TWO CHURCHES

The feudal attack on Irish society came from two allied sources: the Normans and the Church of Rome. Ireland had been Christian for centuries, and was widely famed as a centre of learning and literacy. Students from all over Europe attended Ireland's famous medical and religious schools. Anglo-Saxons, too, went to Ireland to study or pursue the religious life, and, according to Bede, the Irish 'welcomed them all gladly'.[6] Aldfrith, who became king of Northumbria in 685 AD, was educated at Lisgoole, on the banks of the Erne. Irish monks spread Christianity and literacy through the Anglo-Saxon kingdoms, making Lindisfarne and Iona the 'Athens of the North', and founded settlements as far afield as Iceland, Italy and Ukraine.

The Irish Church was based on independent monasteries which held little land, and the early Irish monks were famous for their spirituality, their scholarship and their love of solitary wandering. In mainland Europe the church took a different course. As the feudal system gained ground, the church, based in Rome, followed suit. It became increasingly worldly, and concerned with acquiring land, wealth and power. In England, the Roman system gained the ascendancy after 664, when, at the Synod of Whitby, Roman and Celtic Christians met to discuss their points of difference, and the Roman faction won the day.

Before the Normans invaded Ireland, a movement began within the Irish Church arguing for the adoption of the Roman feudal-style system. In support of their argument, pro-Roman churchmen cited Celtic customs – such as marriage laws which permitted divorce, and allowed a man to marry his deceased brother's wife, which was regarded as incest by Rome – as evidence that the Irish were not true

Page from the Book of Kells, from the beginning of the ninth century

7

Christians. Malachy of Armagh wrote that:

> He discovered it was not to men but to beasts he had been sent; in all the barbarism which he had yet encountered, he had never met such a people so profligate in their morals, so uncouth in their ceremonies, so impious in faith, so barbarous in laws, so rebellious to discipline, so filthy in life, Christian in name but Pagans in reality.[7]

But Malachy did not go unchallenged. When he started building a large church at Bangor, one inhabitant protested that it was a needless frivolity, for 'we are Irish not Gauls.'[8]

The Normans, who began invading Ireland in 1169, echoed Malachy's sentiments, and presented their invasion as a religious mission. King Henry II obtained the papal blessing for the conquest. In 1172, Pope Alexander III wrote that he had heard how Henry had conquered 'with God's aid, that Irish people, who put aside the fear of God and wander unbridled through the rough and dangerous ways of vice', and urging Henry 'to recall the Irish, through your power, to the observance of the Christian faith'.[9]

Such justifications of conquest or persecution on religious grounds were common in Europe. The Crusades, aimed at acquiring plunder and at securing the trade routes to the east, were conducted in the name of capturing the Holy Places in Jerusalem. In England, the Crusades were followed by a pogrom against the Jews, which led, in 1190, to the deaths of 150 Jews in York.

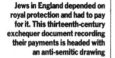

Jews in England depended on royal protection and had to pay for it. This thirteenth-century exchequer document recording their payments is headed with an anti-semitic drawing

Right: The Tara brooch, made in about 700 AD of bronze overlaid with gold, amber and glass

GERALD OF WALES

The Norman view of the Irish was to cast a long shadow over English perceptions. This was due, in large part, to the writings of Gerald of Wales, a churchman of mixed Norman-Welsh ancestry. Gerald's family were Norman Marcher Lords, and were deeply involved in the invasions of Ireland. He first travelled to Ireland in 1183 and again in 1185, this time in the service of King Henry II, acting as tutor to Henry's son John. In his works on Ireland, Gerald aimed to glorify the Norman conquest.

Gerald's *History and Topography of Ireland*, dedicated to Henry, was divided into three parts.[10] The first part described the geography of Ireland and its flora and fauna; the second part described 'wonders and miracles' – such as 'a fish with three gold teeth'; while the third part described the inhabitants of Ireland and their history.

While Gerald praised the natural riches of Ireland, he wrote contemptuously of the people, portraying them as inferior to the Normans in almost every respect. He regarded their pastoral (herding) economy as inferior to settled agriculture: 'They live on beasts only, and live like beasts. They have not progressed at all from the habits of pastoral living.' He condemned their customs, citing their dress and also 'their flowing hair and beards' as examples of their 'barbarity'. Their backwardness was, he said, because of the remoteness of Ireland, which meant that they were 'cut off from well-behaved and law-abiding people'.

Though Gerald had a few good words for the Irish clergy, he vilified the religious practices and marriage customs of the people:

Illustrations from manuscripts of Gerald's works on Ireland

> This is a filthy people, wallowing in vice. Of all peoples it is the least instructed in the rudiments of the faith. They do not yet pay tithes or first fruits or contract marriages. They do not avoid incest.

His ferocity was probably in part explained by his need to undermine the widespread view of Ireland as a centre of Christianity and civilisation.

He also wrote that the Irish were treacherous and deceitful, breaking their pledges. As historian Robert Bartlett has pointed out, the Anglo-Norman view of the Irish and Welsh as treacherous probably derives from the fact that the native peoples found it expedient to make temporary surrenders or agreements, but when circumstances changed and the enemy's position weakened, they would reassert their independence.[11]

Gerald did, however, single out one aspect of Irish life for praise. Like later generations of colonisers, in Ireland and elsewhere, he was willing to acknowledge the artistic skills of the colonised: 'It is only in the case of musical instruments,' he wrote, 'that I can find any commendable diligence in the people. They seem to me to be incomparably more skilled in these than any other people I have seen.'

The Irish evidently regarded the Normans' claims of superiority with some scepticism. Gerald records how a senior Irish churchman, the archbishop of Cashel, responded to the accusation that Ireland had failed to produce any martyrs:

> 'It is true,' he said, 'that although our people are very barbarous, uncivilised, and savage, nevertheless they have always paid great honour and reverence to churchmen, and they have never put out their hands against the saints of God. But now a people has come to the kingdom which knows how, and is accustomed, to make martyrs. From now on Ireland will have its martyrs, just as other countries.'

It was a prophetic remark.

Gerald's work was to have a baleful influence on English attitudes for several centuries. Initially his work reached a very restricted audience: he wrote in Latin, his age lacked printing, and literacy was confined to a few. But in later centuries his influence spread. His work was published in English in the Elizabethan era, when further attempts were being made to subjugate Ireland, and was very well received, since it tallied with the anti-Irish prejudices of the time.

Gerald's contention that the Irish were a barbaric people complemented English colonial ambitions, and for almost seven centuries his work was quoted by historians as fact.[12] The seventeenth century Irish historian Séathrún Céitinn complained:

> Every one of the new Galls who writes on Ireland writes in imitation of Cambrensis [Gerald]... because it is Cambrensis who is as the bull of the herd for them for writing the false history of Ireland, wherefore they had no choice of guide...[13]

The Normans denigrated all the Celtic peoples. These thirteenth-century drawings show an Irishman (below left) and a Welshman (below right)

Ireland in about 1500, showing the Pale and the areas controlled by Irish chiefs, some of them descended from Normans

BEYOND THE PALE

The Normans' attempt to conquer Ireland and establish feudalism was less successful than their conquest of England. The Celts proved more difficult to subdue than the more centralised and sedentary Anglo-Saxons, and the great distances involved made it difficult to enforce submission.

While some Celtic rulers accepted King Henry's overlordship, they continued with their Gaelic customs and were unwilling to pay tribute. The Normans were not racist in the modern sense, and many of the colonists were rapidly assimilated into the local populace, with Norman lords becoming Celtic-style chieftains.

The area over which English kings had full control was centred on Dublin and was known as 'the Pale'. The Pale fluctuated dramatically in size in different periods. The word 'pale' means boundary, and the phrase 'beyond the Pale' was to become established in the English language, meaning 'uncivilised' and 'socially unacceptable'.

By 1250 the Anglo-Normans controlled about three-quarters of Ireland, but from then on their power declined. The Irish, allied with gaelicised Normans, fought back fiercely. By the fourteenth century, Normans outside the Pale had merged with the native Irish to such an extent that the English tried to stop the process by enacting apartheid-style laws. The Statutes of Kilkenny of 1366 forbade intermarriage between the Anglo-Normans and the Irish, banned religious bodies in English-controlled areas from accepting Irish people, banned the settlers from speaking Irish and receiving Irish entertainers, and prohibited the adoption of Irish dress, and customs such as the sport of hurling.

But such laws were ineffective in the face of the Gaelic resurgence. The Irish – with the exception of some who stood to gain from the conquest – fought back both physically and ideologically, refusing to accept either Anglo-Norman rule or Anglo-Norman values. In the fourteenth century, for instance, Irish leaders complained to Pope John XXII that the Irish 'have been depraved, not improved, by intercourse with the English, who have deprived them of their ancient written laws.'[14]

Right: Extract from the Brehon laws, from the Book of Ballymote of about 1400

12

THE
KINGDOME
OF IRLAND
Deuided into seuerall Prouinces, and the
againe deuided into Counties.
Newly described.

The Gentleman of Ireland · The Gentlewoman of Ireland

The Ciuill Irish Woman · The Ciuill Irish man

The Wilde Irish man · The Wilde Irish Woman

Iodocus Hondius cælauit

THE TUDOR COLONISERS

During succeeding centuries, the relationship between the English ruling class and the Irish people remained fundamentally the same. The English continued to try to subjugate Ireland, while the Irish continued to resist. Consequently the derogatory stereotype of the Irish, which derived from and justified English colonial exploits, was kept alive, taking on new characteristics according to the pre-occupations of each age.

The reconquest of Ireland began under the Tudor monarchs in the sixteenth century. It was during this period that England began to develop into a nation in the modern sense, and English nationalism was born. The aristocracy was by now English rather than French, and English had become the official language. The church, too, was 'nationalised': the Papacy, a foreign power, was ejected, and the church was made subservient to the state. The Church of England, however, still defined itself as Catholic – though 'reformed' – rather than Protestant. The monarchy developed alliances with the rising merchant class, offering protection in return for money.

The Tudor monarchs sought to incorporate the Celtic countries on England's borders – Cornwall, Wales, Ireland and Scotland – within the boundaries of the state. In turn, the conquest of the Celtic regions was the first step towards English territorial expansion across the Atlantic.

PLANTATIONS

England's rulers wanted to control Ireland primarily for strategic reasons. Ireland had become a base from which both claimants to the English throne and also hostile European powers – notably Spain – could organise opposition.

In Mary Tudor's reign, the English adopted the policy known as 'plantation', which involved driving the native Irish off their land and replacing them with English settlers. The planters came to Ireland lured by the promoters' promise that 'You may keep a better house in Ireland for £50 a year than in England for £200 a year'.[15] The Irish resisted, and the latter half of the sixteenth century saw ferocious and almost continuous war, which left large tracts of Ireland devastated. In Elizabeth's reign, of the total of just under £5 million spent on foreign wars, nearly half went for the Irish wars.

The colonisers' methods were brutal in the extreme. In 1574, for example, an expedition to Ulster organised by the Earl of Essex slaughtered the entire population of Rathlin Island, some 600 people of Scottish origins. Edward Barkley, a member of the expedition, gave a graphic description of how Essex's men had driven the Irish from the plains into the woods, where they would freeze or die of hunger with the onset of winter, and concluded, 'how godly a deed it is to overthrow so wicked a race the world may judge: for my part I think there cannot be a greater sacrifice to God.'[16]

When the Irish in Munster resisted colonisation, they were met by total war. Sir Humphrey Gilbert, the military governor of Munster and half-brother of Sir Walter Ralegh stated:

> I slew all those from time to time that did belong to, feed, accompany or maintain any outlaws or traitors; and after my first summoning of a castle or fort, if they would not presently yield it, I would not take it afterwards of their gift, but won it perforce – how many lives soever it cost; putting man, woman and child to the sword.[17]

The pamphleteer Thomas Churchyard, who accompanied Gilbert to Munster, justified the killing of non-combatants on the grounds that they provided food for the rebels, 'so that the killing of them by the sword was the way to kill the men of war by famine.' Churchyard gave a vivid description of Gilbert's methods:

> that the heads of all those (of what sort soever they were) which were killed in the day, should be cut off from their bodies and brought to the place where he encamped at night, and should there be laid on the ground by each side of the way leading into his own tent so that none could come into his tent for any cause but commonly he must pass through a lane of heads which he used *ad terrorem*, the dead feeling nothing the more pains thereby; and yet did it bring great terror to the people when they saw the heads of their dead fathers, brothers, children, kinsfolk and friends, lie on the ground before their faces, as they came to speak with the said colonel.[18]

ELIZABETHAN PREJUDICES

The Elizabethan years produced, in the words of historian Nicholas Canny, 'an outpouring of justifications for colonisation and conquest.'[19] In 1577 the first histories of Ireland written in English appeared, in the first volume of Holinshed's *Chronicles*. The histories, by Edmund Campion and Richard Stanyhurst, depicted the Irish as a barbarous and backward people.

The Gentleman of Ireland

The Civill Irish man

The wilde Irish man

Included in the same volume was the first English translation of the work of the Norman writer Gerald of Wales.[20] The various justifications for colonisation were brought together and elaborated by Edmund Spenser, the poet and author of *The Faerie Queene*, in his book *A View of the State of Ireland*, which was published in 1596. Spenser spent 18 years in Ireland, amassing considerable property in County Cork, and fled the country when his castle – purloined from the locals – was burned to the ground in the Munster rebellion of 1598.

The English colonists justified their actions by arguing that the Irish were culturally inferior to themselves, and that the English would civilise them. They condemned Irish religious practices, criticising them more for failing to practise Catholicism properly than for their rejection of Protestantism. Spenser wrote that the Irish 'all be papists by their profession, but in the same so blindly and brutishly uninformed (for the most part) that not one amongst a hundred knoweth any ground of Religion, or any Article of his faith'.[21] Barnaby Rich, an English army captain who arrived in England in 1573 and was later associated with the colonisation of Ulster, declared, 'They are more foolish, superstitious in Ireland than they can be in Rome itself.'[22]

As further evidence of Irish backwardness, the English cited their pastoral farming methods, which involved moving with the seasons, as well as their Gaelic customs – the Brehon laws, their poets, their dress and hairstyles, and not least their violent resistance. The Elizabethans classified the Irish as 'barbarians', who had missed out on the supposed benefits of Roman colonisation, and frequently likened them to other peoples whom they also saw as 'barbarous'. One Elizabethan versifier wrote:

Figures illustrating an English map of Ireland made in 1616, part of which is shown on the previous pages

Gentlewoman of Ireland

The Civill Irish Woman

The Wilde Irish Woman

17

Two woodcuts from Elizabethan illustrator John Derrick's 'Image of Irelande', published in 1581. Above: The Elizabethans defamed the Irish in order to justify the conquest – note the two figures on the right preparing to defecate. Below: English soldiers return from a battle bringing Irish heads.

Wild Irish are as civil as the Russies in their kind,
Hard choice which is the best of both, each bloody, rude and blind.[23]

And in his book *A New Description of Ireland*, published in 1610, Barnaby Rich wrote:

> The time hath been, when they lived like *Barbarians*, in woods, in bogs, and in desolate places, without politic law, or civil government, neither embracing religion, law or mutual love.
>
> That which is hateful to all the world besides is only beloved and embraced by the Irish, I mean civil wars and domestical dissensions.
>
> The wild uncivil *Scythians*, do forbear to be cruel the one against the other. The *Cannibals*, devourers of men's flesh, do learn to be fierce amongst themselves, but the *Irish*, without all respect, are ever more cruel to their very neighbours.[24]

Edmund Spenser held similar views:

> Marry those be the most barbaric and loathy conditions of any people (I think) under Heaven… They do use all the beastly behaviour that may be, they oppress all men, they spoil as well the subject, as the enemy; they steal, they are cruel and bloody, full of revenge, and delighting in deadly execution, licentious, swearers and blasphemers, common ravishers of women, and murderers of children.[25]

Spenser attributed this supposed depravity to the effects of Irish customs and traditions, especially the Brehon laws. He put forward a line of argument that was to become familiar in Britain's later colonial exploits. He argued that it would be folly to govern the Irish by the laws of the English constitution, since this would allow them to retain their customs and rebel again in the future. Rather, Gaelic law should be forbidden and the Irish should be subjected by force. Spenser advocated the occupation of all of Ireland, an increased military effort against the 'woodkernes' or guerrilla fighters, and the creation of protected hamlets where the captured Irish would be given land to farm, educated to Christian values and protected from the guerrillas. Only then, he declared, could the Irish be brought 'from their delight of licentiousness and barbarism into love of goodness and civility.'

A VALE OF TEARS

Most of the Irish, for their part, evaluated their culture, and England's role, very differently. One sixteenth century poet, writing in Irish, praised a young warrior who was true to his traditions:

> Eoghan Bán, the darling of noble women,
>   A man who never loved English customs,
> Does not set his heart on English ways,
>   but rather has chosen the wild life.
>
> Little he cares for gold-embroidered cloaks,
>   or for a high well-furnished ruff,
> Or for a gold ring that would only be vexatious,
>   or for a satin scarf down to his heels.[26]

Another Derrick woodcut, with the original accompanying verses

A   Here creepes out of Sainct Filchers denne, a packe of prowling mates, Most hurtfull to the English pale, and noysome to the states: Which spare no more their country byrth, then those of th'english race, But yeld to each a lyke good turne, when as they come in place.

B   They spoyle, and burne, and beare away, as fitte occasions serve, And thinke the greater ill they doe, the greater prayse deserve:

   They passe not for the poore mans cry, nor yet respect his teares, But rather joy to see the fire, to flash about his ears. To see both flame, and smouldring smoke, to duske the christall skyes, Next to their pray, therein I say, their second glory lyes.

C   And thus bereaving him of house, of cattle and of store: They do returne backe to the wood, from whence they came before.

The Irish writer Séathrún Céitinn wrote caustically of the English historians:

> I think it is not allowable they should have the repute of historians... as it is almost according to the fashion of the dung beetle they act when writing about the Irish. For it is the fashion of that beetle not to stoop towards any flower... or any blossom in the garden, but it keeps bustling about until it meets with dung of horse and cow, and proceeds to roll itself therein. [27]

Many Irish people doubtless shared the sentiments of another Gaelic poet, whose words were also later translated into English:

> May we never taste of death nor quit this vale of tears
> Until we see the English go begging down the years;
> Packs on their backs to earn a penny pay,
> In little leaking boots as we went in our day.
>
> Time has o'erthrown, the wind has blown away
> Alexander, Caesar, such great names as they.
> See Troy and Tara where in grass they lie –
> So even the very English yet might die! [28]

Spaniards hanging Indians and setting fire to their houses, in an engraving by reformer Bartolomé de las Casas

THE AMERICAS

In developing ideas about the cultural inferiority of the Irish, the English were following in the footsteps of the Spanish, who used similar ideas about the native peoples of the Caribbean and South America to justify a conquest of unparalleled brutality. The English colonisers were familiar with the Spaniards' notions, and may have been influenced by them. [29] It was the Spanish, too, who led the way in the trans-Atlantic slave trade. Those Spaniards who opposed the maltreatment and extermination of the native South Americans advocated replacing them with African labour, and by the mid-sixteenth century the Spaniards were importing thousands of African slaves every year.

The colonisation of Ireland was the prelude to English colonisation of America. Indeed, the first attempts at establishing settlements in America were made by people such as Sir Walter Ralegh and Sir Humphrey Gilbert who had been in the forefront of the colonisation of Ireland. The American colonists regarded the native people in much the same way as they had regarded the Irish, and English writers frequently compared them. The same pretexts were used for the extermination of the native Americans as had been used in the 1560s and 1570s for the slaughter of the Irish. Historian Nicholas Canny writes:

> At first the English claimed their mission to be that of civilising the native

inhabitants... When relations between the English and the Indians grew tense, emphasis was given to the barbaric traits of the native population. After the Indian insurrection of 1622 we find the colonisers exulting in the fact that they were now absolved from all restraints in dealing with the Indians.[30]

England's involvement in slaving also began in the Elizabethan period. The first English slave-raiding expedition set off for West Africa in 1562 with the backing of Queen Elizabeth I. The first discriminatory law against black people in England was passed in 1596, when Elizabeth instructed that the 'divers blackamoors' then in the country 'should be sent forth the land'.[31] The subsequent development of the slave trade gave a massive impetus to racism, as Europeans sought to justify their appalling treatment of their African victims.

Above: European print of the native American uprising of 1622. Below: A 1638 illustration of the raid by New England colonists in which 500 Pequot men, women and children were burned alive

THE FLIGHT OF THE EARLS

At the very end of Elizabeth's reign, the power of the Celtic lords was finally broken. In the 1590s, the lords of the northern province of Ulster rose against England, inspiring risings throughout Ireland. Then in 1601 Lord Mountjoy won a decisive victory over the Irish forces and their Spanish allies at the battle of Kinsale. In 1603 the Ulster lords submitted. Too proud to become servants of the English crown, they went into voluntary exile in Italy in 1607. Their departure – known as 'the flight of the earls' – left the way clear for the colonisation of Ulster, which was to be the most thorough of the plantations.

Sir John Davies, Ireland's Attorney-General, exulted over the flight of the earls, and looked forward optimistically to the future:

we hope His Majesty's [James I's] Government will work a greater miracle in this kingdom than ever St Patrick did; for St Patrick did only banish the poisonous worms, but suffered the men full of poison to inhabit the land still; but His Majesty's blessed genius will banish all those generations of vipers out of it, and make it, ere long, a right fortunate island.[32]

Heading of a page in the Council Book of the town of Galway in 1632. The scribe's use of Celtic interlace decoration shows that this style survived for centuries

The Irish, of course, saw the matter very differently. Séathrún Céitinn, in a poem written in Gaelic and recently translated by Thomas Kinsella,[33] lamented the fate of the great families of Ireland. He used various poetic names to refer to Ireland: Fal's high plain, the *lios* of Cobhthach, and the plain of Lugh.

> At the news from Fal's high plain I
>   cannot sleep.
> I am sick till doom at the plight of its
>   faithful folk.
> Long have they stood as a hedge
>   against hostile trash
> but a lot of the cockle has grown up
>   through them at last.
>
> Any worthless crew that thought to
>   cross the sea
> to the fair, gold, age-old *lios* of
>   Cobhthach 'the just'
> – theirs without struggle of hands
>   our mighty mansions
> and the choicest swards of our lovely-
>   bordered places.

There's a new sort growing in the plain of Lugh the lithe
who are base by right, though they flourish their 'rolls' on high
– Eoghan's seed exhausted, Tal's blood troubled and broken,
and the youth of Bantsrath scattered in foreign lands.

22

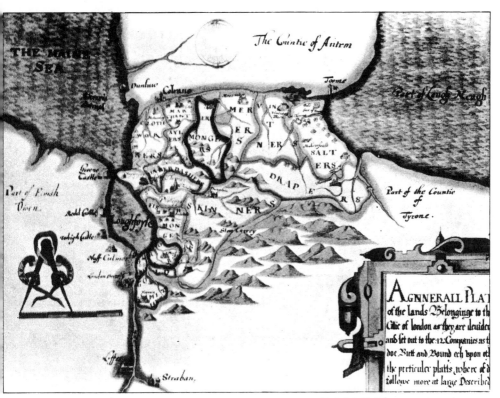

The Countie of Antrim

THE MAIN SEA

Part of Lough Neagh

Part of the Countie of Tyrone.

Part of Enish Owen.

Loughfoyle

Lifer

Straban.

A GNNERALL PLAT of the lands Belonginge to the Citie of london as they are deuided and set out to the 12.Companies as they doe Butt and Bound ech vpon oth the perticuler platts where of d followe more at large Described

Above: A map showing how County Derry was divided among twelve London companies

DISPOSSESSION AND REVOLT

The seventeenth century was to see the almost complete dispossession of the native Irish people, and also of the Old English settlers. In that time, some 85% of their land was expropriated, becoming the property of colonists from England and lowland Scotland.

The 'flight of the earls' in 1607 was followed by the confiscation and plantation of Ulster – the most drastic of the plantations, with repercussions which still affect politics today. County Derry was handed over to a group of London companies, while the easternmost counties, Antrim and Down, were settled by many thousands of Scots. The Scottish settlers were Presbyterians, and, like the Catholic Irish, suffered persecution by the Crown. During the next 150 years, many were to join the exodus to the new colonies in America.

In 1641 the Irish in Ulster, joined by many of the Old English settlers, rose against England hoping to repossess their lands. The leaders of the rising claimed to be acting in support of the English king Charles I. Charles was beleaguered in England by the Puritan parlia-

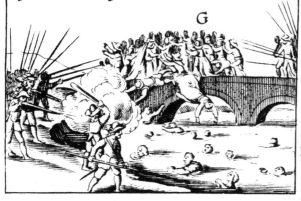

Driuinge Men Women & chidren by hund:
reds vpon Briges & casting them into Riuers,
who drowned not were killed with poles &
shot with muskets.

G

Illustrations from an anti-Catholic pamphlet published in London in 1642 giving a highly exaggerated account of the 1641 rising

mentarians, who were battling to curb the monarchy and win political power for the merchant class and landed gentry. Protestant colonists also formed armies, some supporting the royalists and others supporting parliament.

English writers of the time, such as Sir John Temple, ascribed the 1641 rising not to the grievances of the Irish, but to their supposed backwardness, which, he said, made them unable to understand or appreciate England's efforts to civilise them. The rising was accompanied by atrocities on both sides, but Temple greatly exaggerated those committed by the native Irish. His account did much to inflame English feeling against the Irish, and it made the Irish so indignant that one of the first acts of the Irish parliament of 1689 was to order the book burned by the common hangman.[34]

The Irish rebels were initially successful – by February 1642 almost the whole country was in their hands – but they were gradually driven back by the English forces. Then in August 1649 Oliver Cromwell arrived in Ireland and in a dreadful campaign crushed the Irish and royalist resistance.

CROMWELL

Cromwell's aims were both strategic and economic. He wanted to prevent Ireland from becoming a base for foreign and royalist opposition, and at the same time to make Ireland 'a profitable part of the Commonwealth'.[35]

In the minds of Cromwell and his supporters, the fact that they were both English and Protestant marked them out as superior to the rest of the world's people. 'God is decreeing some new and great period,' wrote the poet John Milton. 'What does he then but reveal himself... as his manner is, first to his Englishmen?'[36]

Christopher Hill, a leading historian, has written, 'A great number of civilised Englishmen of the propertied class in the seventeenth century spoke of Irishmen in tones not far removed from those which Nazis used about Slavs, or white South Africans use about the original inhabitants of their country. In each case the contempt rationalised a desire to exploit.'[37]

Cromwell portrayed his campaign in Ireland as a religious and civilising mission. Before embarking at Bristol, he told his troops that they were Israelites about to enter Canaan and extirpate its idolatrous inhabitants. On arrival, he told the citizens of Dublin that by God's 'divine providence' he and his troops would 'carry on the great work against the barbarous and bloodthirsty Irish, and their adherents and confederates' and so restore 'that bleeding nation to its former happiness and prosperity'.[38]

Cromwell's campaign, however, made Ireland bleed with a vengeance, and reduced many of the population to destitution. At Drogheda – where the garrison was officered by English Catholic royalists – Cromwell's troops massacred the garrison, the clergy and some of the townspeople. They went on to slaughter some 2,000 people at Wexford. Cromwell reported on the killings:

> It hath pleased God to bless our endeavours at Drogheda... The enemy were about 3,000 strong in the town... I do not think 30 of the whole number escaped with their lives. Those that did are in safe custody for the Barbados... I wish that all honest hearts may give the glory of this to God alone, to whom indeed the praise of this mercy belongs... I am persuaded that this is a righteous judgement of God upon those barbarous wretches who have imbrued their hands in so much innocent blood; and that it will tend to prevent the effusion of blood for the future – which are the satisfactory grounds to such actions, which otherwise cannot work but remorse and regret.[39]

A contemporary woodcut of the siege of Drogheda

Cromwellian propaganda – a contemporary broadsheet

THE LEVELLERS

In England there was significant opposition to Cromwell's Irish campaign, even within the ranks of his own army. This came from the radical Leveller movement, who spoke for the English poor and wanted to push the English revolution much further than Cromwell did. Cromwell described the Levellers as 'persons differing little from beasts', and said, 'You must cut these people in pieces or they will cut you in pieces.'[40] In May 1649 some Leveller regiments, inspired by a mixture of political and economic grievances, rebelled. Cromwell swiftly defeated them, and departed for Ireland in August.

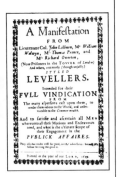

The Levellers sympathised with the Irish rebels and opposed the reconquest of Ireland on principle. William Walwyn said that 'the cause of the Irish natives in seeking their just freedoms... was the very same with our own cause here in endeavouring our own rescue and freedom from the power of our oppressors.'[41]

One of the Leveller leaflets, which incurred the capital penalty for treason for inciting the army to disobedience, asked a series of 18 questions, including these:

Have we the right to deprive a people of the land God and nature has given them and impose laws without their consent?

How can the conquered be accounted rebels, if at any time they seek to free themselves and recover their own?

Whether Julius Caesar, Alexander the Great, William Duke of Normandy or any other great conqueror of the world were any other than great lawless thieves, and whether it be not as unjust to take laws and liberties from our neighbours as to take goods from another of the same nation?

Whether those who pretend for freedom (as the English now) shall not make themselves altogether inexcusable in entrenching upon others' freedoms, and whether it be not the character of a true patriot to endeavour the just freedom of all men as well as his own?

Whether the English would not do as the Irish have, if the Irish should dispossess and tyrannise over them?[42]

The Cromwellians issued an elaborate answer to this leaflet, emphasising repeatedly that the Irish were murderers and must be punished, and saying they were 'more brutish than the Indians' – probably a reference to the native Americans – and that it was the duty of the English to 'tame such wild beasts'.

One Leveller pamphleteer condemned not only 'how the English hunted the poor Irish', but also European commercial expansion in general:

Our merchants, they travel by sea and land to make Christian proselytes, chiefly our Indian merchants; but consider their practices, and the profit that we have by their double dealing, first in robbing of the poor Indians of that which God hath given them, and then in bringing of it home to us, that we thereby may the better set forth and show the pride of our hearts in decking our proud carcasses, and feeding our greedy guts with superfluous unnecessary curiosities.[43]

27

TO HELL OR CONNAUGHT

By 1650 Cromwell had suppressed most of Ireland leaving it in ruins. He then went on to Scotland to suppress the rebellion there. In 1652 and 1653 the English parliament passed some of the most drastic measures in its history: the policy known as 'to Hell or Connaught'.

The English parliament planned to seize three-quarters of Ireland, using the confiscated land to pay Cromwell's soldiers, while the populations of Ulster, Munster and Leinster were to be driven into an area west of the River Shannon consisting of Connaught and County Clare. If they were found east of the Shannon after 1 May 1654, the penalty would be death.

A Gaelic poet wrote a poem, translated by Thomas Kinsella, about the exodus to Connaught;" just as Cromwell saw the English as the Israelites, so the poet saw the Irish as the Israelites, but in a different role:

Ouer-throvv of an

Jrifh rebell,in a late battaile :

Or

The death of Sir *Carey Adoughertie*, who murdred
Sir George Paulet *in Ireland ; and for his re-*
bellion hath his head now ftanding ouer
Newgate in Dublin.

Imprinted at London for I. Wright, and are to be fold at
his fhop neere Chrift Church gate. 1608.

Title page of a book printed in
London in 1608

Consider a parable of this:
    Israel's people, God's own,
although they were in bonds in Egypt,
    found in time a prompt release.

People of my heart, stand steady,
    don't complain of your distress.
Moses got what he requested,
    religious freedom – and from Pharoah.

If they call you 'Papishes'
    accept it gladly for a title.
Patience, for the High King's sake.
    Deo Gratias, good the name!

God who art generous, O Prince of Blessings,
behold the Gael, stripped of authority.
Now as we journey Westward into Connacht
old friends we'll leave behind us in their grief.

Cromwell's plan to clear the Irish into the west did not fully succeed, but his campaign and its aftermath left Ireland devastated. In 1641, Ireland's population had been about 1,500,000: ten years later, it had been halved. Some 616,000 people had died (504,000 Irish people, and 112,000 settlers and troops). About 40,000 more had left to serve in European armies. A further 100,000 people, many of them beggars, had been rounded up and transported to the new colonies in the Caribbean and America as slaves.

Cromwell's Irish policy was part of his general imperial policy: in particular, he planned to follow the conquest and settlement of Ireland with the conquest and settlement of the West Indies. The

The C R U E L
M A S S A C R E
Of the PROTESTANTS, in
North America;
Shewing how the French and Indians
join together to scalp the English, and
the manner of their Scalping, &c. &c.

Printed and Sold in Aldermary Church-Yard,
Bow Lane, L O N D O N.

English already had a foothold in the Caribbean – they had landed in St Kitts and Barbados in the 1620s – and Cromwell's plan, known as the 'Western Design', was to break the Spanish monopoly in the area and establish a permanent base there. In 1655 his troops captured Jamaica, which, as the centre of the slave trade, was to be crucial to British imperial and foreign policy for the next 150 years.

The demand for labour on the plantations prompted mass kidnappings in Ireland. A pamphlet published in 1660 accused the governor of Galway of sending his soldiers out to grab any Irish people they could in order to sell them to Barbados for profit:

> It was a usual practise with Colonel Strubber, the governor of Galway, and other commanders in the said county, to take people out of their beds at night and sell them for slaves to the Indies, and by computation sold out of the said county about a thousand souls.[45]

When soldiers commanded by Henry Cromwell, Oliver's son, seized a thousand 'Irish wenches' to sell them to Barbados, Henry justified the action by saying that 'although we must use force in taking them up', yet it was 'so much for their own good and likely to be of so great advantage to the public'. He also suggested that 2,000 Irish boys of 12 to 14 years could be seized to the same purpose: 'who knows but it might be a means to make them Englishmen...'[46]

The English colonists took their methods from Ireland to the Americas. In Ireland, an English soldier was rewarded with £5 for bringing in the head of a 'rebel' or a priest, and with £6 for a wolf's head. The colonists in New England during their wars against the native Indians in the 1660s and 1670s killed the Indians and cut off their heads, or captured them and sent them to the West Indies as slaves. They also offered bounties to the Indians to bring in the scalps of rival tribes. 'Scalping' saved the trouble of bringing in whole heads. The Indians copied the practice from the whites, and were later wrongly blamed for the idea.[47]

Colonists of all nations oppressed and exploited the native Americans. The colonists introduced and sponsored the practice of 'scalping'. Above: The British accuse the French. Below: Americans accuse the British, during the War of Independence.

Bring me the Scalps
and the King our Master
will reward you

Reward for
16 _ Scalps.

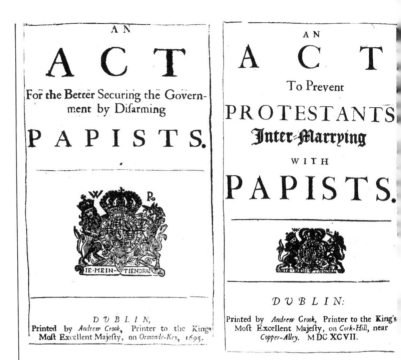

ASCENDANCY

Irish fortunes looked up briefly when the Stuart monarchy was restored to power in England. But then, at the invitation of members of parliament, William of Orange, a Dutch Protestant, became king. The Stuart king, James II, who was allied to France, fled to Ireland. William, backed by the Pope and the king of Spain, followed him there and defeated him in 1690.

Power in Ireland now lay in the hands of a new landowning class, Protestant in religion and English in sympathy, who became known as the 'Ascendancy'. The Catholics – native Irish and Old English settlers – held only 20% of the land and many lived in extreme poverty. The Irish scholar Ruairí Ó Flaihearta wrote: 'I live a banished man within the bounds of my native soil; a spectator of others enriched by my birthright; an object of condoling to my relations and friends, and a condoler of their miseries.'[48]

Under William, only the Church of England was recognised, and both Catholics and Presbyterians were disenfranchised. From 1691 a series of 'penal laws' were passed against them. The penal laws denied Catholics and dissenting Protestants religious freedom, access to education, the right to vote, and all access to government jobs. The laws also drastically curtailed Catholic rights to land, so that by 1775 they held only five per cent of the land in Ireland.

English historians remained obstinately blind to the desolation which English rule had brought to Ireland. Instead, they continued to denigrate the Irish and condemn them for their inability to perceive

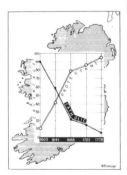

The transfer of land ownership

A N

A C T

To Prevent the

𝔉urt𝔥er 𝔊rowt𝔥

O F

POPERY.

DUBLIN:

Printed by *Andrew Crook*, Printer to the Queen's moſt Excellent Majeſty, on the *Blind-Key*, MDCCIII.

A N

A C T

To Prevent

Popiſh Prieſts

From coming into this

KINGDOM.

DUBLIN:

Printed by *Andrew Crook*, Printer to the Queen's moſt Excellent Majeſty, on the *Blind-Key*, MDCCIII.

Front pages of four of the many penal laws passed against Catholics

the 'benefits' of English government. Richard Cox, in his book *Hibernia Anglicana* which appeared in 1689, portrayed Irish history as a succession of savage acts:

> Feuds continued with the greatest pride, most hellish ambitions and cruellest desires of revenge, and followed with the most horrible injustices, oppressions, extortions, rapines, desolations, perfidious treasons, rebellions, conspiracies, treacheries and murders, for almost two thousand years... That we never read of any other people in the world so implacable, so furiously, so eternally set upon the destruction of one another... the Irish have as much reason to thank God and the English for a more civil and regular government exercised over them.[49]

Nathaniel Crouch, whose history of Ireland appeared in 1693, wrote:

> the English endeavoured to civilize the people, and to introduce the English laws, language, habit and customs among them, thereby to reduce them to civility, yet such was their rough, rebellious disposition, and their implacable malice to the English, that nothing could attemper, or reduce them to any tolerable patience; so that in all times, as well as when they were admitted into the condition of subjects, as while they were esteemed and treated as enemies, they took all advantages, most perfidiously to rise up and imbrue their hands in the blood of their English neighbours, and Ireland hath long continued a true Alcedama, or field of blood, and a dismal sepulchre for the English nation...[50]

DREAMS

The Irish continued to hope for the return of the Stuart kings, and the poets wrote *aisling* poems, which describe a dream in which the poet meets a sad and beautiful woman, who is Ireland, awaiting the return of her Stuart lover who will rescue her from English tyranny. One of the best known early eighteenth century Gaelic poets was Aogán Ó Rathaille, whose *aisling* poem *Brightness of Brightness* was translated by Frank O'Connor:[51]

> Brightness of brightness lonely met me where I wandered,
> Crystal of crystal only by her eyes were splendid,
> Sweetness of sweetness lightly in her speech she squandered,
> Rose-red and lily-glow brightly in her cheeks contended.
>
> There she told me, told me as one that might in loving languish,
> Told me of his coming, he for whom the crown was wreathed,
> Told me of their ruin who banished him to utter anguish,
> More too she told me I dare not in my song have breathed.
>
> Truth of truth I told her in grief that it shamed her
> To see her with a sleek foreign mercenary lover
> When the highest peak of Scotland's race already thrice had named her,
> And waited in longing for his exile to be over.

Anti-Jacobite propaganda – an English playing card of about 1689 depicts James II's viceroy, the earl of Tyrconnell, as the knave

'ALL OUR WEALTH TRANSMITTED'

Ireland became a source of cheap food and raw materials for England – a colonial economy. By the start of the eighteenth century, over £1 million in rent was leaving Ireland each year for the pockets of absentee landlords in Britain, and by the middle of the century about one third of Ireland's produce was leaving the country in this way. Trade to Ireland was the most important branch of England's overseas trade. Irish industries which competed with British products were suppressed, and Ireland was forbidden to trade with other British colonies. The English demand for beef led to the clearing and de-population of vast areas of land.

For the Irish peasantry, the results were disastrous. They lived in squalid poverty unparalleled in Europe. Famine was endemic. After a famine in 1727, Jonathan Swift, the Anglican dean of St Patrick's Cathedral in Dublin and author of *Gulliver's Travels*, wrote two bitter pamphlets. The first was titled *A Short View of the State of Ireland*, echoing the title of Edmund Spenser's book. He wrote:

> One third part of the rents of Ireland is spent in England which, with the profits of employments, pensions, appeals ... and other incidents, will amount to a full half of the income of the whole kingdom, all clear profit to England... The rise of our rents is squeezed out of the very blood, and vitals, and clothes, and dwellings of the tenants, who live worse than English beggars...[52]

Swift wrote that a stranger taking a journey through Ireland

> would be apt to think himself travelling in Lapland or Iceland, rather than in a country so favourable by nature as ours... The miserable dress, and diet, and dwelling of the people; the general desolation in most parts of the kingdom; the old seats of the nobility and gentry all in ruins and no new ones in their stead; the families of farmers who pay great rents living in filth and nastiness upon buttermilk and potatoes, without a shoe or stocking to their feet, or a house so convenient as an English hogsty to receive them – these may, indeed, be comfortable sights to an English spectator who comes for a short time to learn the language, and returns back to his own country, whither he finds all our wealth transmitted.[53]

'A MODEST PROPOSAL'

In 1729 Swift wrote his famous and macabre satire, *A Modest Proposal*, in which he again tried to draw attention to the horrific condition of the Irish poor.[54] The pamphlet, ostensibly written by a 'projector' or planner, put forward a scheme for solving Ireland's economic problems by fattening up the children of the poor and selling them as meat:

> I have been assured by a very knowing American of my acquaintance in London; that a young healthy child, well nursed, is at a year old, a most delicious, nourishing and wholesome food; whether stewed, roasted, baked or boiled; and, I make no doubt, that it will equally serve in a fricasie or ragoust...
>
> I grant this food will be somewhat dear, and therefore very proper for

33

landlords; who, as they have already devoured most of the parents, seem to have the best title to the children.

The scheme has numerous advantages, including that 'it would greatly lessen the number of Papists, with whom we are yearly over-run; being the principle breeders of the nation, as well as our most dangerous enemies'. Further:

> we can incur no danger in disobliging England: for, this kind of commodity will not bear exportation; the flesh being of too tender a consistence, to admit a long continuance in salt; although, perhaps, I could name a country, which would be glad to eat up our whole nation without it.

TEAGUELAND JESTS

To the English upper and middle classes, however, the Irish peasantry were, literally, a joke. Anti-Irish jokes, or 'Irish bulls', were so commonplace that collections of them appeared in book form. A 'bull' is defined by the Oxford Dictionary as 'a self-contradictory proposition', or 'an expression containing a manifest contradiction in terms or involving a ludicrous inconsistency unperceived by the speaker.'

Joke books often appeared under the name 'Joe Miller': a name signifying comics in general. The Joe Miller book of 'Teagueland Jests and Bog Witticisms', published in 1749, was prefaced with the words:

> The bulls and witticisms that too frequently drop from Irish mouths have made them the discourse and entertainment of all sorts of companies. Nothing more recommends Teague and his countrymen than their natural stupidity.[55]

The jokes were identical in theme to those in circulation today. There was one about the Irishman who said, 'No English hen ever laid a fresh egg.' And the one about the Englishman who asked how far it was from Waterford to Cork. Paddy thought for a while, then answered: 'Be Chreesht! I cannot tell dee how many miles it is from Waterford to Cork – but it is about ayteen milesh from Cork to Waterford.'

To combat the ubiquitous jokes the Anglo-Irish writer Maria Edgeworth, author of *Castle Rackrent* and other novels, and her father Richard Lovell Edgeworth, wrote their *Essay on Irish Bulls*. This was first published in 1802, and ran to several editions. The Edgeworths dissected the question with wit and irony, marshalling numerous

In order to justify English dominance, the Scots, too, were depicted as backward. This print from the time of the 1745 Jacobite rising shows a highlander unable to comprehend 'civilised' conveniences. After the rising, the English banned highland dress and the clans were driven from their lands

KNAVISH PAT——A TALE.

An Irish-man came late unto an Inn,
And ask'd the Maid what Meat there was within.
"Cow-heels," she answer'd, "and a Breast of Mutton.
"Then, quoth the Irish man, "as I'm no glutton.

Either of these will serve; to night the Breast,
The Heels i'the morning... then light Meat is best.
If Night he took the Breast, and did not pay,
I'the Morning took the Heels, and ran away.

Publish'd May 7 1804. by LAURIE & WHITTLE, 53 Fleet Street, London.

An anti-Irish cartoon published in London in 1804

examples to demonstrate that many 'Irish' jokes were originally told about other peoples, and that stories of English idiocy can also be told. They observed: 'It was formerly in law no murder to kill a *merus Hibernicus*; and it is to this day no offence against good manners to laugh at any of this species.'[56]

By this time, too, the 'stage Irishman' had become a familiar figure in the theatre. The first known example is Shakespeare's foolish and temperamental Captain Macmorris in *Henry V*, which was written in 1598. Macmorris's behaviour accorded with the description given by his fellow officer, the Welshman Fluellen: 'By Cheshu, he is an ass, as in the world... he has no more directions in the true disciplines of the wars, look you, of the Roman disciplines, than is a puppy-dog.'

For the next 300 years, both Anglo-Irish and English playwrights portrayed the Irish as either ingratiating rogues – lazy, cunning and often drunk – or as braggarts, often ex-soldiers boasting of imaginary exploits. Such roles were often filled by Irish actors, seeking to make a living by parodying their own people.

35

A crew of pirates are driven by a storm they know not whither, at length a boy discovers land from the topmast, they go on shore to rob and plunder; they see an harmless people, are entertained with kindness, they give the country a new name, they take formal possession of it for the King, they set up a rotten plank or a stone for a memorial, they murder two or three dozen of the natives, bring away a couple more by force for a sample, return home, and get their pardon. Here commences a new dominion acquired with a title by divine right. Ships are sent with the first opportunity, the natives driven out or destroyed, their princes tortured to discover their gold; a free licence given to all acts of inhumanity and lust, the earth reeking with the blood of its inhabitants: and this execrable crew of butchers employed in so pious an expedition, is a modern colony sent to convert and civilise an idolatrous and barbarous people.

JONATHAN SWIFT
'Gulliver's Travels'

CONCEALING REALITY

Such stereotypes of the Irish helped to justify England's exploitation of Ireland. The notion that the English were superior and the Irish were buffoons echoed, at the level of popular entertainment, the intellectuals' contention that English rule was beneficial to the backward Irish. This view, of course, served to conceal the fact that in reality English rule, as Swift had pointed out, was of immense benefit to England and a disaster for Ireland. It was much more convenient to believe that Irish poverty was the fault of the Irish themselves.

British intellectuals continued to paint a derogatory picture of the Irish. The Scottish philosopher David Hume urged the government 'to abolish the Irish customs which supplied the place of laws, and which were calculated to keep the people forever in a state of barbarism and disorder.'[57] In his very influential *History of England*, which was published in the 1750s and ran through 36 editions in the next hundred years, Hume described Irish history in the same terms as had Spenser and other English historians:

> The Irish from the beginning of time had been buried in the most profound barbarism and ignorance; and as they were never conquered or even invaded by the Romans, from whom all the western world derived its civility, they continued still in the most rude state of society, and were distinguished by those vices alone to which human nature, not tamed by education, or restrained by laws, is for ever subject.[58]

Hume contended that the Irish had remained Catholic after the reformation because their 'rudeness and ignorance... were extreme' and

> they were sunk below the reach of curiosity and love of novelty by which every other people in Europe had been seized at the beginning of the century... The ancient superstitions... mingled and polluted with many wild opinions, still maintained an unshaken empire over them; and the example alone of the English was sufficient to render the reformation odious to the prejudices of the discontented Irish. The old opposition of manners, laws and interests was now inflamed by religious antipathy, and the subduing and civilising of that country seemed to become every day more difficult and impracticable.[59]

IRISH CHALLENGES

The eighteenth century saw increasing numbers of Irish people, both Protestant and Catholic, challenging such accounts of Irish history and the defamatory stereotypes of the Irish. This process was part of a more general movement of the upper classes in Ireland to assert their rights against Britain. Like the colonists in America, who declared their independence in 1776, they chafed against the political and economic restrictions imposed by Britain. In 1798 the United Irishmen rose in rebellion: Britain savagely suppressed the rising, then bribed the Irish parliament into dissolving itself and accepting the Act of Union in 1800.

The Dublin-born political philosopher Edmund Burke, whose wife and mother were Catholic and father Protestant, inspired a circle of historians to re-evaluate Irish history. 'If it can be shown,' wrote Burke, 'that the great rebellions of Ireland have arisen from attempts to reduce the natives to the state to which they are now reduced, it will show that an attempt to continue them in that state will rather be disadvantageous to the public peace than any kind of security to it.'[60]

One of Burke's protegees was John Curry, a Catholic, whose history was published in 1775. In the introduction, he attacked British historians:

> For a dark and disgraceful century had Irish history been looked upon as a register of the crimes of the Irish people. The calumny of Temple, Borlace, Cox, Campion and Carew, had become the popular belief in England. They were woven into the history of Hume, and acquired all the permanence and currency which a polished style and philosophical appearance would bestow. Hence a system of plunder and persecution, organised into a code of laws, was excused, for defended it could not be... Insult was added to outrage. The Irish were considered scarcely human, and inhuman indeed was the system by which they were oppressed.[61]

An illustration from an Irish magazine depicting a scene from the 1798 rising: the British hang a piper for playing seditious tunes

petit Souper. a la Parisienne __ or __ A Family of Sans Culotts refreshing after the fatigues of the day.

Among those who challenged the stereotypes of the Irish was the great English agriculturalist Arthur Young. In his book *A Tour in Ireland*, published in 1780, he wrote:

It is an illiberal business for a traveller to sit down coolly in his closet and write a satire on the inhabitants of a country. Some persons have given a very gross misrepresentation of the Irish nation. Many strokes in their character can be ascribed to the extreme oppression under which they live. There are no people but might be better than they are found, and none but have virtues which deserve attention at least as much as their failings...[62]

One English traveller who particularly incensed the Irish was Richard Twiss, whose bestselling book, *A Tour of Ireland*, was published in 1775. This contained observations such as:

What little the men can obtain by their labour or the women by their spinning is usually consumed in whiskey, which is a spirituous liquor resembling gin.

They seem to form a distinct race from the rest of mankind. As to the natural history of the Irish species, they are only remarkable for the thickness of their legs especially those of the plebian female.[63]

A Dublin potter responded to these calumnies by producing a chamber pot with Twiss's likeness painted on the bottom, so that, in the words of writer Mary Campbell, 'indignant Irish readers could freely express their opinion of his book.'

38

NO PEOPLE MORE PREJUDICED

English contempt for the Irish was part of an increasingly entrenched disdain for foreigners in general, and visitors from other countries often remarked on this trait. The Swiss traveller de Saussure observed in 1727:

> I do not think there is a people more prejudiced in its own favour than the British people, and they allow this to appear in their talk and manners. They look on foreigners in general with contempt, and think nothing is as well done elsewhere as in their own country.[64]

The English upper classes also had little time for the English working class. Discussing the end of the eighteenth century, historian J.H. Plumb wrote that 'It was a general conviction that the working man was a savage, unprincipled brute'.[65]

English people commonly ascribed their supposed superiority to their 'blood' or ancestry. Daniel Defoe lampooned this notion in his poem *A True-born Englishman*,[66] which was published in 1701, and proved very popular, quickly running through numerous editions. Defoe wrote the poem in defence of King William of Orange, who was being criticised because he was Dutch. The preface began:

> The intent of the satyr is pointed at the vanity of those who talk of their antiquity, and value themselves upon their pedigree, their ancient families, and being True Born; whereas 'tis impossible we should be True Born; and if we could, should have lost by the bargain.

In the poem, Defoe enquired into 'old Britannia's youthful days', listing the diverse peoples who had settled in England:

Irish illustrations of British atrocities following the 1798 rising. Above: Pitch-capping. Below: A travelling gallows

The Romans first with Julius Caesar came,
Including all the Nations of that Name,
Gauls, Greeks, and Lombards; and by
    Computation,
Auxiliaries or Slaves of ev'ry Nation.
With Hengist, Saxons; Danes with Sueno
    came,
In search of Plunder, not in search of Fame.
Scots, Picts and Irish from th' Hibernian
    Shore:
And Conqu'ring William brought the
    Normans o're.

All these their Barb'rous Offspring left
    behind,
The Dregs of Armies, they of all Mankind;
Blended with Britains who before were here,
Of whom the Welsh ha' blest the Character.

From this Amphibious Ill-born Mob began
That vain ill-natur'd thing, an Englishman.

THE SLAVE TRADE

English vanity and arrogance grew as England fought off the competition from other European countries and became the world's leading trading nation, going on to industrialise rapidly. The key to England's prosperity was the trade with the colonies, and in particular the trade in African slaves.

Initially, agricultural labour in the Caribbean was supplied by transported Europeans: deportees, convicts and indentured labourers were brought from Ireland, Scotland and England itself. But by the end of the seventeenth century the system of white labour was breaking down. The whites were generally freed after three to ten years, and given plots of land, but as the plantations swallowed up the available land, the 'poor whites' were left destitute. Increasingly the planters turned to a new source of labour – slaves from Africa, who remained slaves for life.[67]

In the eighteenth century, the development of the plantations in the Caribbean and America prompted a huge growth in the slave trade, with some 60,000 Africans being carried across the Atlantic each year. England became the main European slaving nation, deriving enormous profits from the 'triangular trade': manufactured goods were taken to Africa and exchanged for captured Africans, who were taken to the West Indies and exchanged for food and raw materials.

HORROR ALMOST INCONCEIVABLE

The slaves, unlike slaves in earlier types of societies, had no rights

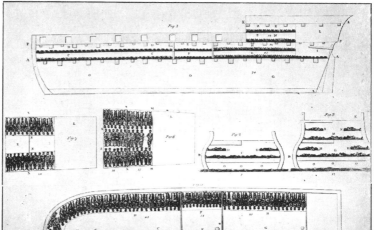

Plan of a slave ship showing how Africans were stowed on the Atlantic crossing

A branding iron used to brand traders' initials on slaves

at all and were treated as commodities. They were advertised for sale alongside horses and other goods. Olaudah Equiano, who was kidnapped from his home in Nigeria at the age of 11 and transported to the West Indies, and eventually became a leader of Britain's black community, recalled the terrible 'middle passage' from Africa to the Caribbean:

> I was soon put down under the decks, and there I received such a salutation in my nostrils as I had never experienced in my life: so that, with the loathsomeness of the stench, and crying together, I became so sick and low that I was not able to hear, nor had I the least desire to taste any thing. I now wished for the last friend, death, to relieve me...
>
> I had never seen among any people such instances of brutal cruelty; and this not only shewn towards us blacks, but also to some of the whites themselves...
>
> This wretched situation was again aggravated by the galling of the chains, now become insupportable; and the filth of the necessary tubs, into which the children often fell, and were almost suffocated. The shrieks of the women, and the groans of the dying rendered the whole a scene of horror almost inconceivable.[68]

The Europeans justified their barbarous behaviour by turning logic on its head, arguing that they were 'civilised' while the Africans were 'savages'. Early European visitors had been awed by the magnificence of the great African civilisations. When the Dutch visited the West African city of Benin at the start of the eighteenth century they recorded:

> The town seems to be very great. When you enter into it, you go into a great broad street, not paved, which seems to be seven or eight times broader than the Warmoes street in Amsterdam...
>
> The king's palace is a collection of buildings which occupy as much space as the town of Harlem... There are numerous apartments for the Prince's ministers and fine galleries, most of which are as big as those on the Exchange at Amsterdam. They are supported by wooden pillars encased with copper, where their victories are depicted, and which are carefully kept very clean.
>
> The town is composed of thirty main streets, very straight and 120 feet wide, apart from an infinity of small intersecting streets. The houses are close to one another, arranged in good order. These people... wash and scrub their houses so well that they are polished and shining like a looking-glass.

But this view of Africa did not suit the requirements of the slave trade.

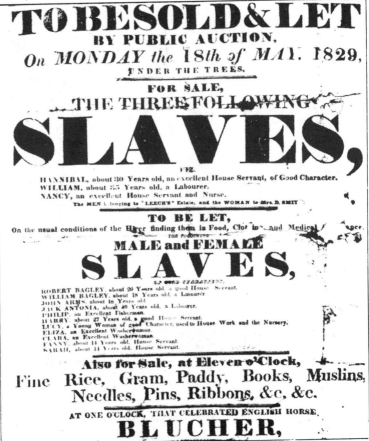

The British denigrated the Africans in terms similar to those they used about the Irish, but even more defamatory. While the Irish were despised for their 'inferior' brand of Christianity, the Africans were dismissed for not even being Christians, but 'heathens'. And African customs were represented as even more 'barbaric' than those of the Irish. Further, the Africans were dark-skinned – and black was a colour which had very negative associations in the white European Christian tradition.

The eighteenth century philosopher David Hume, who wrote so contemptuously of the Irish, also maligned the Africans. In an infamous footnote to his essay *Of National Characters* he wrote:

> I am apt to suspect the negroes, and in general all the other species of men (for there are four or five different kinds) to be naturally inferior to the whites. There never was a civilised nation of any other complexion than white, or even any individual eminent in either action or speculation. No ingenious manufacture amongst them, no arts, no sciences. On the other hand, the most rude and barbarous of the whites, such as the ancient Germans, the present Tartars, have still something eminent about them…[69]

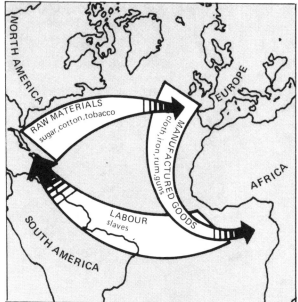

This view, of course, provided a convenient rationale for maintaining the highly profitable institution of slavery. As the French philosopher Montesquieu sarcastically said: 'it is impossible to allow that negroes are men; because if we allow them to be men, it will begin to be believed that we ourselves are not Christians.' Ottobah Cugoano, who was kidnapped in Ghana at the age of 13 and taken to the West Indies, then brought to England and freed, commented bitterly on the double standards of British law-makers, asking:

> Is it not strange to think, that they who ought to be considered as the most learned and civilised people in the world, that they should carry on a traffic of the most barbarous cruelty and injustice, and that many... are become so dissolute as to think slavery, robbery and murder no crime?[70]

Those who opposed the institution of slavery also argued against the view that Africans were innately inferior. The campaigner

Thomas Clarkson responded to David Hume by citing the names of former slaves who had succeeded in various fields, and observed:

> If the mind of the African were unbroken by slavery, if they had the same expectations in life as other people, and the same opportunities for improvement... they would be equal, in the various branches of science, to the Europeans... the argument that states them 'to be the inferior link of the chain of nature, and designed for servitude', as far as it depends on the *inferiority* of their capacities, is wholly malevolent and false.[71]

In the English view of the world, the Irish occupied a position way below themselves, but just above the Africans. The two were often compared, as in these verses from *Punch* in 1848:[72]

Six-foot Paddy, are you no bigger –
You whom cozening friars dish –
Mentally, than the poorest nigger
Grovelling before fetish?

You to Sambo I compare
Under superstition's rule
Prostrate like an abject fool.

THE RAJ

The British similarly denigrated the inhabitants of other parts of their expanding empire. When the first English trading enclaves were established in India, the traders, according to historian J.H. Plumb, made 'a genuinely self-interested attempt to make themselves agreeable to the Indians.' They adopted Indian food and dress, and often married Indian women. 'They were traders,' writes Plumb, 'proud of their race, determined to make money as fast as they could, but they were wholly free from the sense that manifest destiny had called them to rule the native people.'[73]

But as British political power was consolidated, the British Raj became increasingly arrogant. By the end of the eighteenth century, all Indians were excluded from posts in government service, and British society became increasingly isolated and bigoted. The British justified the Raj by arguing that the Indians were 'heathens' and 'backward' and therefore unfit to rule themselves. In 1813 Lord Hastings, displaying total ignorance of Indian society and history, wrote:

> The Hindoo appears a being nearly limited to mere animal functions and even in them indifferent. Their proficiency and skill in the several lines of occupation to which they are restricted, are little more than the dexterity which any animal with similar conformation but with no higher intellect that a dog, an elephant or a monkey, might be supposed to be capable of attaining. It is enough to see this in order to have full conviction that such a people can at no period have been more advanced in civil policy.[74]

46

'THE MOST OFFENSIVE DOCUMENT'

As the coffers of British traders and industrialists filled at the expense of the colonised peoples, British self-esteem continued to swell. The historian Thomas Babington Macaulay boasted that the British 'have become the greatest and most highly civilised people that ever the world saw', and in 1834 he made the notorious comment that 'a single shelf of a good European library' was 'worth the whole native literature of India and Arabia'.[75] The poet laureate, Lord Tennyson, echoed him:

> Thro' the shadow of the globe we sweep into the younger day:
> Better fifty years of Europe than a cycle of Cathay.[76]

Such racist attitudes found their most vicious expression in the work of the historian Thomas Carlyle, a proto-fascist who was totally opposed to liberty, democracy and equality either within or outside Britain. His infamous *Occasional Discourse on the Nigger Question*, published in 1849, was described by the late Eric Williams, historian and prime minister of Trinidad and Tobago, as 'the most offensive document in the entire world literature on slavery and the West Indies.'

Carlyle argued that the recently emancipated slaves should be forced to work for the whites:

> decidedly you will have to be servants to those that are born *wiser* than you, that are born lords of you; servants to the Whites, if they are (as what mortal can doubt they are?) born wiser than you.[77]

He caricatured them malevolently: 'With a pennyworth of oil, you can make a handsome glossy thing of Quashee, when the soul is not killed in him. A swift, supple fellow; a merry-hearted, grinning, dancing, singing, affectionate kind of creature...'

Carlyle also vilified the Irish, whom he detested. He visited the country soon after the famine, and filled his journal with invective against what he called this 'brawling unreasonable people'. Ireland,

Children's jigsaw puzzle produced in London in about 1850

THE SUGAR PLANTATION.

he wrote, was a 'huge suppuration', a 'human swinery', 'an abomination of desolation', and 'a black howling Babel of superstitious savages'.[78]

FAMINE AND DIASPORA

All over the globe, British imperial expansion left destitution in its wake. In Ireland, famine succeeded famine, culminating in the 'Great Hunger' of 1845 to 1849, in which one-and-a-half million people died of starvation and disease, while a further million emigrated.

This was no 'natural' disaster: Ireland produced enough food to feed the starving people, but the peasants had to sell it to pay their rent, and throughout the famine ships left Ireland laden with grain, barley, oats and cattle. John Mitchel, a leader of the revolutionary Young Ireland movement, stormed in despair:

Irish drawing showing depopulation in the years after the Great Hunger

> immense herds of cattle, sheep and hogs… floating off on every tide, out of every one of our thirteen seaports, bound for England; and the landlords were receiving their rents and going to England to spend them; and many hundreds of poor people had laid down and died on the roadsides for want of food.[79]

In India, where Britain followed the same policy of crushing native industry and forcing the peasants to produce for export, the results were the same. The second half of the nineteenth century saw more than 20 million Indians die of famine, while many others were exported as semi-slave labour to the West Indies, Malaysia and Africa. As in Ireland, too, there were frequent revolts and uprisings against the British.

The famine in Ireland gave a massive impetus to the diaspora that had been taking place for centuries. From the days of the Elizabethan conquests, migration became a way of life – it is conservatively estimated that today 24 million people living throughout the world could claim Irish nationality. Precluded from using their talents in their native country, many Irish emigrants became prominent figures in their new homelands. Some became presidents, prime ministers, or millionaires, while others became labour leaders or revolutionaries. Their descendants included people as different as John F. Kennedy and Ernesto Che Guevara – whose father's surname was Lynch.

We entered a cabin. Stretched in one dark corner, scarcely visible from the smoke and rags that covered them, were three children huddled together, eyes sunk, voice gone, and evidently in the last stage of actual starvation. . . .

Crouched over the turf embers was another form, wild and all but naked, scarcely human in appearance. Moaning piteously was a shrivelled old woman, begging us to give her something, partly baring her limbs to show how the skin hung loose from her bones. . . .

We visited over fifty of these tenements. The scene was one and invariable, differing little but in number of sufferers. They did but rarely complain. When asked what was the matter, the answer was alike in all: 'Thá shein uchrais' ('I am hungry'). We truly learned the meaning of that sad word 'uchrais'.

WILLIAM BENNETT, a visitor to north Mayo, 1847

48

PORT OF LIMERICK.

SHIPPING INTELLIGENCE.

ARRIVED

Ann Moore, M'Fie, Quebec, timber.
Jane, Mulcahy, St. John's, do.
Moy, O'Grady, do. do.
Expedition, Raymond, Glasgow, railway iron.
Thetis, Hughill, Quebec, timber.

SAILED

Jane Black, Gorman, Quebec, emigrants.
Cleofrid, Leark, do. ballast.
Moodkee, Viggors, do. do.
Freights to London.—28 0d per quarter oats; Liverpool and Clyde, 7s per ton.

IMPORTS.

Ann & Elizabeth from Windau—1474 pieces timber.
Earl of Devon from Ancona—899 7-8 rubbers of Indian corn Harvey Brothers.
Roberts from Miramichi—62 tons timber, 3360 pieces deals, Alexander Brothers.
Governor from Quebec—200 tons timber, 3 M pipe. 4 M bri staves, 39½ hund deals, F Spaight. *Energy* from do.—19 loads timber, 30 3 5 deals, 28 3 26 staves J Harvey & Co.
Bryan Abbs from do.—186 pieces timber, 26 2 14 staves, 29 0 20 deals, F Spaight. *Oberon* from do. for Clare—220 loads timber.
MacNamara & Son; 20 0 1 pieces deals, 15 1 20 staves. *Lady Lilford* from do. for Clare—50 loads timber, 20 3 13 pieces deals, 3 fathom lathwood, MacNamara & Son. *Harriet* from do. for Clare—29 loads timber, 28 … deals, 2 fm … lathwood, James B … matyne.

EXPORTS.

Ann for London—150 firks butter, Edwards & Barry; 200 do J Edwards; 200 do. M O'Donnell; 313 do. 100 firks 10 casks lard, … Christie ; 15 … do. J Sheehy ; 250 do. T M'Donnell ; 500 do. C Nash & Son ; 100 do. M Hurley ; 300 do. 3 casks hams, P Ryan ; 63 do. A J Yielding ; 81 bales bacon, 6 … firks 3 casks lard, J Harley & Son ; 50 do. 20 casks lard, A Russell & Co ; 52 bris pork, Shaw & Duffield ; 60 bales bacon, J & P M'Donnell ; 39 puns whiskey, J Sharp ; 76 bales bacon, 21 casks hams, 4 crates hair, J Russell ; 264 bris oats, … bert …

Messenger for London—1150 bris oats, T W … all.
Pethan Clinton for Liverpool—725 b … ats, … Her-725 do. M … R. Wheeler ;
City of Limerick for Glasgow—40 tons flour, J N Russell ; 50 bales bacon, 200 kegs lard, A Russell & Co.
British Queen for Glasgow—500 bris wheat, T Worrall & Co; 128 do. T Worrall ; 450 do. oats, J & T Myles.
John Guise for London—1663 bris oats, T M Usborne.
Cambrian Maid for Glasgow—1000 bris barley, J Denniston & Co.
Marianne for Tralee—300 sacks Indian meal, J N Russell.

STRUGGLES OF AN OPPRESSED PEOPLE

A small minority of English people, including members of the radical Chartist movement and a few prominent intellectuals such as the economists George Poulett Scrope and John Stuart Mill, saw that the poverty and violence in Ireland was the result not of Irish 'backwardness' but of British exploitation. In a pamphlet first published in 1834, Scrope urged the government to curb the nearly absolute powers of the landlords if it wished to avert starvation and revolution:

> It is impossible… to have any doubt as to the real cause of the insurrection
> ary spirit and agrarian outrages of the Irish peasantry. They are the
> struggles of an oppressed starving people for existence! They are the rude
> efforts at obtaining a sort of savage self-established justice… They are the
> natural and necessary results of a state of law which allows the landlords of
> a country at one time to encourage an excessive growth of population on
> their estates, and at another, when caprice seizes them, to dispossess all
> this population, and turn them out on the highways without food and
> shelter.[80]

But most British politicians, newspaper editors and intellectuals remained resolutely blind to the connection between British policy and conditions in Ireland. Rather, they contended that Irish poverty and violence were the fault of the Irish themselves, the result of deficiencies in the Celtic character which marked them out as inferior. The British, on the other hand, were portrayed as paragons of virtue. The young Benjamin Disraeli declared in an article in the Times in 1836 that the Irish

> hate our free and fertile isle. They hate our order, our civilisation, our
> enterprising industry, our sustained courage, our decorous liberty, our

pure religion. This wild, reckless, indolent, uncertain and superstitious race has no sympathy with the English character...[81]

Fraser's magazine, popular with the English middle classes, expounded in 1847 on the differences between the English and the Irish:

> The English people are naturally industrious – they prefer a life of honest labour to one of idleness. They are a persevering as well as energetic race, who for the most part comprehend their own interests perfectly, and sedulously pursue them. Now of all the Celtic tribes, famous everywhere for their indolence and fickleness as the Celts everywhere are, the Irish are admitted to be the most idle and the most fickle. They will not work if they can exist without it.[82]

The Times asked the same year, 'What is an Englishman made for but for work? What is an Irishman made for but to sit at his cabin door, read O'Connell's speeches and abuse the English?'[83]

It was even claimed that the Irish were content with their poverty – a convenient argument that absolved Britain of any responsibility for mitigating the effects of the famine. Blackwood's Magazine pontificated in 1846 that 'The truth is... that though there is much more squalid filth and raggedness in Ireland (for those are national tastes) there is much less real misery or distress in that country than exists in England.'[84] The same year, the Times made this utterly callous comment:

> For our own part we regard the potato blight as a blessing. When the Celts once cease to be potatophagi, they must become carnivorous. With the taste of meats will grow an appetite for them; with the appetite, the readiness to earn them.[85]

THE IRISH REVOLUTION, AT LAST! OR MILESIAN MORALFORCE VERSUS PHYSICAL FORCE!

An English cartoon of 1840 portrays the followers of Daniel O'Connell and the Young Irelanders fighting each other

THE IRISH OGRE FATTENING ON THE FINEST PISANTRY.

'SAVAGE TRIBES'

Just as the British upper classes saw Irish poverty as stemming from Celtic idleness, so they saw Irish violence as resulting from a Celtic taste for anarchy. In British minds, poverty and agrarian violence were unconnected. In a book published in 1824, a traveller wrote of the Irish that

> Their very amusements are polemical: fighting is a pastime which they seldom assemble without enjoying... When not driven by necessity, they willingly consume whole days in sloth, or as willingly employ them in riot...[86]

A cartoon from Punch in 1846 attacking the radical Young Ireland movement

In 1844 another traveller declared that 'The murders of this country would disgrace the most gloomy wilds of the most savage tribes that ever roamed in Asia, Africa or America.'[87] And in 1846 the Times concluded that Irish violence defied explanation:

> An Irishman commits a murder as a Malay runs a-muck. In certain circumstances it is expected of him, and he would be thought a mean and spiritless wretch if he demurred at it. It is only unfortunate that these circumstances are so indefinite. The conditions under which a Malay draws his krise for the last rush, like those which dictate self-immolation in Japan, are pretty well known by all persons conversant with the native character, and precautions can sometimes be taken against the catastrophe. Even in Madrid and Venice, the insults to be washed out only by blood were defined with some precision. But it is impossible to catalogue the offences which among Irishmen entail sudden murder or secret assassination.[88]

Two English cartoons attacking Daniel O'Connell. Below: In 1845, during the famine, O'Connell is obscenely portrayed as 'the real potato blight of Ireland'

Refusing to admit that the Irish had genuine grievances, the British vilified even Daniel O'Connell's Repeal movement, which aimed for reform and used constitutional methods. In one article alone, the Times in 1836 described O'Connell as 'scum condensed of Irish bog', 'a greedy self-serving Satan', and a man 'whose principles we hold in abhorrence, as those of the worst being in human form that ever disgraced the floor of an English senate.'[89] O'Connell was portrayed as exploiting the child-like Celts for his own selfish ends. The Times said in 1843:

> A people of acute sensibilities and lively passions, more quick in feeling wrongs than rational in explaining or temperate in addressing them – as easily roused into outrage by supposed oppression as subdued into docility by felicitous kindness – equally susceptible of gratitude for hypocritical sympathy as of indigation at unintentional or imaginary injury – no less impetuous in repaying the one than ardent in avenging the other – such is the people whose virtues and vices... O'Connell has so fiendishly exploited.[90]

DOUBLE STANDARDS

The notion that the Irish were inferior to themselves provided the British with a convenient excuse for applying different standards of justice in Ireland than they would at home. Since the Act of Union in 1800, the two countries had become one political unit, the United Kingdom. But while Ireland was subject to coercive laws and a repressive administration, Britain was not. The British justified the discrepancy by arguing that the Irish were uncivilised and un-English. The Times pronounced in 1846:

> The great obstacle to tranquillity in Ireland is the national character – the character of the masses, of the middle classes, of the senators of Ireland... When Ireland acts according to the principles of civilised man, then she can be ruled by the laws of civilised man.[91]

That Britain's subjugation and exploitation of Ireland was far more 'uncivilised' than anything the Irish had done was of course not considered.

Some months later the Times expanded on the theme:

> To Englishmen a vigour beyond the Consititution is an odious thing. The powers granted by the Constitution they have always found adequate to meet emergency and danger. And it seems unkind and unjust to recommend for Irishmen a policy that would be scouted for ourselves. But we must be ruled by circumstances. If crimes are un-English – if English means for detecting and punishing them fail, why should not an un-English power be exercised in districts where violence and murder stalk unavenged and unchecked?[92]

Such attitudes remain all too evident in Britain's handling of the situation in the North of Ireland today.

'SCIENTIFIC' RACISM

By the mid-nineteenth century, Britain controlled large parts of the world directly – Ireland, the British West Indies, Canada,

The Victorians justified imperialism by portraying all the peoples whom they wished to rule as backward. In this Punch cartoon of 1853, the Chinese are shown as blocking the path to progress

Harper's Weekly

IRISH IBERIAN.   ANGLO–TEUTONIC.   NEGRO.

The Iberians are believed to have been originally an African race, who thousands of years ago spread themselves through Spain over Western Europe. Their remains are found in the barrows, or burying places, in sundry parts of these countries. The skulls are of low, prognathous type. They came to Ireland, and mixed with the natives of the South and West, who themselves are supposed to have been of low type and descendants of savages of the Stone Age, who, in consequence of isolation from the rest of the world, had never been out-competed in the healthy struggle of life, and thus made way, according to the laws of nature, for superior races.

Australia, South Africa, India – and exercised indirect control over even vaster areas. Then one country after another was annexed, till by the end of the century the British empire was estimated to comprise a quarter of the world's land area and a fifth of its population.

The empire was acquired through violence, bribery and the 'divide-and-rule' strategy, but the Victorians attributed their success to 'Anglo-Saxon superiority'. This old idea was now increasingly seen in terms of new pseudo-scientific theories of race.

Discredited by later generations of scientists, nineteenth century theorists divided humanity into 'races' on the basis of external physical features. These 'races' were said to have inherited differences not only of physique, but also of character. These 'differences' allowed the 'races' to be placed in a hierarchy: needless to say the Teutons, who included the Anglo-Saxons, were placed at the top, black people – especially 'Hottentots' – at the bottom, and Celts and Jews somewhere in between.

Anthropologists went around measuring people's skulls, and as-signing them to different 'races' on the basis of factors such as how far their jaws protruded. Celts and others were said to have more 'primi-tive' features than Anglo-Saxons. The physician John Beddoe in-vented the 'index of nigrescence', a formula to identify the racial components of a given people. He concluded that the Irish were darker than the people of eastern and central England, and were closer to the aborigines of the British Isles, who in turn had traces of 'negro' ancestry in their appearances. The British upper classes also regarded their own working class as almost a race apart, and claimed that they had darker skin and hair than themselves.

The Anglo-Saxon character that came in a package with the refined features said to be industrious, thoughtful, clean, law-abiding and emotionally restrained, while the characters of the various colon-ised peoples were said to be the very opposite. The anatomist Robert Knox, in a book published in 1850, described the Celtic character as: 'Furious fanaticism; a love of war and disorder; a hatred for order and

THE FENIAN-PEST.

Hibernia. "O MY DEAR SISTER, WHAT *ARE* WE TO DO WITH THESE TROUBLESOME PEOPLE?"
Britannia. "TRY ISOLATION FIRST, MY DEAR, AND THEN——"

The rise of the revolutionary Fenian movement in the 1860s provoked a spate of vicious cartoons. In this 1866 Punch cartoon, Sir John Tenniel draws Britannia stamping on rebellion and protecting Hibernia from the Fenians. Tenniel was taken on by Punch after illustrator Dicky Doyle left in protest over the paper's anti-Catholic views

patient industry; no accumulative habits; restless, treacherous and uncertain: look at Ireland…' He drew the inevitable political conclusion: 'As a Saxon, I abhor all dynasties, monarchies and bayonet governments, but this latter seems to be the only one suitable for the Celtic man.'[93]

In 1873 a certain Edward Hamilton told his family that he was going to Ireland. His uncle wrote at once to warn him not to bring back an Irish wife: 'The whole nation lies and that is not a good quality in a wife.'[94]

The Victorian upper class men who controlled politics and business were opposed to self-determination not only for the Irish and other colonised peoples, but also for women, and they ascribed similar characteristics to each. The Celts were repeatedly described as a 'feminine' race, while the Anglo-Saxons were regarded as 'masculine' – and therefore the natural rulers. Contrasts were also drawn between the 'soft' Irish Celts of the south and west of Ireland and the 'masculine' Scots-Irish of Ulster.

The poet and critic Matthew Arnold believed that the sensibility of the Celtic nature, 'its nervous exaltation', had a feminine quality: 'The Celt is thus peculiarly disposed to feel the spell of the feminine idiosyncrasy; he has an affinity to it; he is not far from its secret.'[95] In 1882, an Anglo-Irishman remarked that Europe was divided into two sexes, the male and the female countries. Among the latter were Italy and the Celtic countries, which had the 'soft, pleasing quality and charm of a woman, but no capacity for self-government.'

The assorted English prejudices about the Irish were by now embedded in the language. The word 'Irish' itself had a number of derogatory meanings: 'to weep Irish' meant to pretend sorrow; 'to go to an Irish wedding' meant to empty a cesspool; and 'to get up one's Irish' meant to display one's anger. The word 'Paddy', which had been used as a generic term for the Irish since at least the last half of the eighteenth century, was used, as it sometimes still is today, to mean a temper tantrum. 'Paddywhack' was another term for a fit of anger, while a police van became a 'Paddywagon', indicating the widespread association of the Irish with crime. The Irish were also called 'Micks', or 'Mickeys', and 'to take the mickey' is still used to mean to make fun of somebody.

FOUNDERS OF FASCISM

Leading European historians propounded theories which, like those of their scientific colleagues, were the precursors of the fascist ideology of Hitler's Third Reich. British historians claimed that the English were a homogeneous people descended from the Anglo-Saxons, whose Teutonic or Germanic racial heritage gave them a unique capacity for governing themselves and others. The historian Lord Acton wrote in 1862:

> The Celts are not among the progressive, initiative races, but among those which supply the materials rather than the impulse of history, and are either stationary or retrogressive. The Persians, the Greeks, the Romans and the Teutons are the only makers of history, the only authors of advancement. Other races possessing a highly developed language, a speculative religion, enjoying luxury and art, attain to a certain pitch of cultivation which they are unable either to communicate or to increase. They are a negative element in the world... The Chinese are a people of this kind... So the Hindoos... So the Slavonians... To this class of natives also belong the Celts of Gaul... The Celts of these islands, in like manner, waited for a foreign influence to set in action the rich treasure which in their own hands could be of no avail...

With these assumptions, it was easy to justify appropriating other countries and destroying their independence. Acton continued:

> Subjection to a people of a higher capacity for government is of itself no misfortune; and it is to most countries the condition of their political advancement... Theorists who hold it to be a wrong that a nation should belong to a foreign State are therefore in contradiction with the law of civil progress...[96]

Many politicians shared these perceptions. In 1886 Lord Salisbury opposed Home Rule for Ireland with the words: 'You would not confide free representative institutions to the Hottentots, for instance.' Self-government, he concluded, worked well only for people of the 'Teutonic race'.[97] Nor were leaders of the British political left immune from such racist thinking. While staying in Dublin in 1892, the Fabians Beatrice and Sidney Webb wrote to a friend:

> We will tell you about Ireland when we come back. The people are charming but we detest them, as we should the Hottentots – for their very virtues. Home Rule is an absolute necessity in order to depopulate the country of this detestable race.[98]

One of the most ardent proponents of the theory of Anglo-Saxon racial supremacy was James Anthony Froude, a professor of history at Oxford and a disciple of Carlyle. Froude described the Irish country-folk as 'more like squalid apes than human beings', and, as an evangelical Protestant, despised the 'idolatrous Catholics' and their church. He depicted the Irish as 'unstable as water', while the English stood

A Tenniel cartoon from Punch in 1867

E FENIAN GUY FAWKES.

for order and self-control. Only 'efficient military despotism' could succeed in Ireland, he wrote, because the 'wild Irish' understood only force.[99]

Like Carlyle, Froude was interested in the West Indies, and looked back longingly to the days of slavery. He considered the 'negroes', like the Irish, to be an inferior race, and wrote:

> Nature has made us unequal, and Acts of Parliament cannot make us equal. Some must lead and some must follow, and the question is only of degree and kind… Slavery is gone… but it will be an ill day for mankind if no one is to be compelled any more to obey those who are wiser than himself…[100]

Some writers pursued the notion of a biologically defined hierarchy of human races to its limit: the 'final solution'. Charles Dilke, who divided humanity into the 'dearer races', such as the Anglo-Saxons, and the 'cheaper races', such as the Irish and the Chinese, viewed the disappearance of the American Indians with equanimity: 'The gradual extinction of the inferior races is not only a law of nature but a blessing to mankind.'[101] An editorial in the Times in 1865 noted contentedly that 'Celts' were leaving Ireland and being replaced by 'Saxons': the rich and fertile country was 'being cleared quietly for the interests and luxury of humanity… A Catholic Celt will soon be as rare on the banks of the Shannon as a Red Indian on the shores of the Manhattan.'[102]

The historian Edward Freeman, who, as his obituary in the Manchester Guardian put it, 'gloried in the Germanic origin of the English nation', wrote during a visit to America in 1881:

> This would be a grand land if only every Irishman would kill a negro, and be hanged for it. I find this sentiment generally approved – sometimes with the qualification that they want Irish and negroes for servants, not being able to get any other.[103]

From Punch, 31 December 1881: Tenniel shows Father Time introducing Mr Punch to the Irish dynamiter, the latest addition to his waxworks collection which is made up of annual imperial 'problems'

Opposite page: 'The Irish Frankenstein' by Matt Morgan, published in the English weekly Tomahawk in 1869

TIME'S WAXWORKS.

[1881 *JUST ADDED TO THE COLLECTION*]
M. P. "HA! YOU'LL HAVE TO PUT HIM INTO THE CHAMBER OF HORRORS!"

TWO FORCES.

Tenniel shows Britannia protecting Hibernia and wielding the sword of justice against the Irish Land League, in this Punch cartoon of 29 October 1881. Many of the League's leaders, including Parnell, had recently been arrested

'HUMAN CHIMPANZEES'

From the 1860s onwards, the debate among scientists about the relationship of humans to animals prompted British racists to make frequent comparisons between Irish people, black people and apes. The Cambridge historian and novelist Charles Kingsley, author of *The Water Babies*, wrote to his wife from Ireland in 1860:

> I am haunted by the human chimpanzees I saw along that hundred miles of horrible country… to see white chimpanzees is dreadful; if they were black, one would not see it so much, but their skins, except where tanned by exposure, are as white as ours.[104]

The first live adult gorilla arrived in London Zoo in 1860, provoking intense interest as Victorians flocked to see their closest relative. Humourists seized on the event, and in 1862 Punch published a satire titled 'The Missing Link', attacking Irish immigration. Impoverished Irish people had been coming to Britain in search of work since at least the eighteenth century, and had built, among other things, Britain's network of canals. The 'Great Hunger' had forced a massive exodus from Ireland, and racism against Irish immigrants was rampant in England and Scotland. The Punch satirist wrote:

Above: A Victorian cartoon during the Zulu wars attacking the Zulu leader Cetshwayo. The Russian bear is shown inciting him to violence. Below: A photograph of Cetshwayo

A gulf, certainly, does appear to yawn between the Gorilla and the Negro. The woods and wilds of Africa do not exhibit an example of any intermediate animal. But in this, as in many other cases, philosophers go vainly searching abroad for that which they could readily find if they sought for it at home. A creature manifestly between the Gorilla and the Negro is to be met with in some of the lowest districts of London and Liverpool by adventurous explorers. It comes from Ireland, whence it has contrived to migrate; it belongs in fact to a tribe of Irish savages: the lowest species of Irish Yahoo. When conversing with its kind it talks a sort of gibberish. It is, moreover, a climbing animal, and may sometimes be seen ascending a ladder laden with a hod of bricks.

The Irish Yahoo generally confines itself within the limits of its own colony, except when it goes out of them to get its living. Sometimes, however, it sallies forth in states of excitement, and attacks civilised human beings that have provoked its fury.[105]

The Victorians' obsession with their ape-relatives coincided with the rise of the revolutionary Fenian movement, which was dedicated to liberating Ireland through force of arms and returning the land to the people. The Fenians launched raids on police stations in Ireland and bombings in Britain, and British cartoonists represented them as ape-like monsters threatening British civilisation. Cartoonists like the famous Sir John Tenniel, who drew for Punch, portrayed noble Britannia protecting the delicate and dependent Hibernia from the Fenian beast.

One of the minority in Britain who understood that the Fenian movement was the product of British rule, not Irish irrationality, was the political economist John Stuart Mill. He protested against the uninformed reaction in Britain to the Fenian rebellion:

> Alas for the self-complacent ignorance of irresponsible rulers, be they monarchs, classes or nations! If there is anything sadder than the calamity itself, it is the unmistakable sincerity and good faith with which numbers of Englishmen confess themselves incapable of comprehending it. They know not that the disaffection, which neither has nor needs any other motive than aversion to the rulers, is the climax of a long growth of disaffection arising from causes that might have been removed. What seems to them the causelessness of the Irish repugnance to our rule, is the proof that they have almost let pass the last opportunity they are ever likely to have of setting it right.[106]

Tenniel depicts Charles Stewart Parnell as the creator of the monster of Irish agrarian war in this 1882 Punch cartoon

THE IRISH FRANKENSTEIN.

"The baneful and blood-stained Monster * * * yet was it not my Master to the very extent that it was my Creature? * * * Had I not breathed into it my own spirit?" * * * (*Extract from the Works of* C. S. P-RN-LL, M.P.)

By this time, about half of Ireland was owned by only 750 landlords. Irish tenants were evicted with increasing frequency: 2,100 families were evicted in 1880 alone. These conditions led to mass protests led by the Land League, accompanied by increasingly bitter agrarian warfare in which some landlords were assassinated. British cartoonists responded by depicting the Land League's supporters with ape-like faces, huge mouths and sharp fangs. And as the constitutional agitation of the Irish Home Rule Party in parliament became more militant, Home Rule leader Charles Stewart Parnell and his supporters were portrayed with ape-like features.

The Irish, of course, saw matters in a different light. In the satirical magazines read by Ireland's middle and upper classes, it was the Irish – the Home Rule leaders and tenant farmers – who appeared as handsome and honest, while John Bull and his minions – Orangemen, policemen and officials – looked cruel and ugly. Though Irish cartoonists did not generally portray the British as apes, they occasionally did so specifically in order to mock British cartoonists' views of the Irish.

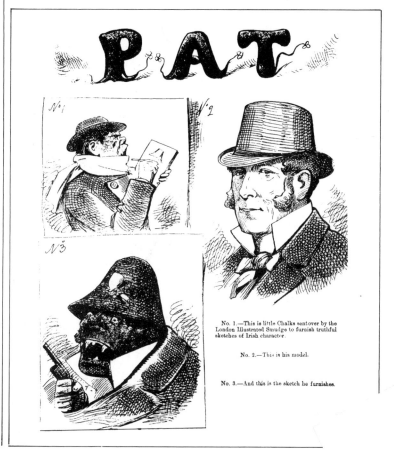

No. 1.—This is little Chalks sent over by the London Illustrated Smudge to furnish truthful sketches of Irish character.

No. 2.—This is his model.

No. 3.—And this is the sketch he furnishes.

An Irish cartoonist mocks the way English artists depict the Irish as monsters, in the Irish magazine Pat in 1881

For centuries, English governments had attempted to buttress their power by destroying the cultures and languages of Ireland, Scotland and Wales. As an official report about Wales put it in 1840: 'a band of efficient schoolmasters is kept up at a much less expense than a body of police or soldiery'.[107] A campaign to save the Irish language was begun by Northern Protestants in the eighteenth century, but when the 'national' education system – later described by the poet-revolutionary Pádraic Pearse as 'the murder machine' – was introduced in 1831, Irish had no place and rapidly declined. The growth of the nationalist campaign in the last half of the nineteenth century was accompanied by an awakening of interest and pride in Ireland's past and in the Gaelic language, and numerous cultural organisations were established. As a result of widespread agitation, Irish was eventually introduced to the syllabus, though only as an optional subject, in 1878.

The upsurge of Irish pride was strongly reflected in the theatre. In the manifesto for the Abbey Theatre, founded in 1898, the poet William Butler Yeats wrote, 'Our theatre will show that Ireland is not the home of buffoonery and easy sentiment as it has been represented.' And the leading playwright John Millington Synge wrote:

> It should never be forgotten that half the troubles of England and Ireland have arisen from ignorance of the Irish character, ignorance based on the biased view of... historians, and on the absurd caricatures which... have achieved much in the way of making the Irish character a sealed book to the Englishman.[108]

'A BREAD AND BUTTER QUESTION'

Ironically, the dramatic expansion of the empire in the last decades of the nineteenth century was in fact a symptom of Britain's decline from its former status as the world's top imperialist power. Other European countries and the United States were now overtaking Britain economically, and the fierce scramble for colonies was the result.

For the British ruling class, the empire was a life-line. Cecil Rhodes, diamond millionaire, prime minister of the Cape and coloniser of Rhodesia, said in 1895:

> In order to save the 40,000,000 inhabitants of the United Kingdom from a bloody civil war, we colonial statesmen must acquire new lands to settle

A stick which Irish schoolchildren had to wear round their necks: every time the child spoke in Irish, a notch was carved on the stick, and at the end of the day the child was punished for each offence. A similar device was used in Wales and Scotland

the surplus population, to provide new markets for the goods produced by them in the factories and mines. The Empire, as I have always said, is a bread and butter question. If you want to avoid civil war, you must become imperialists.[109]

As Britain's downhill slide accelerated, British self-esteem paradoxically reached an all-time high. As historian Bernard Porter has described it, Britain in the 1890s 'became an "imperialistic" power in a self-conscious kind of way she had not been before... flaunting her empire like a cock-bird blowing up his feathers to assert his dominance to rivals.' Thus Lord Rosebery reflected: 'How marvellous it all is! Built not by saints and angels, but the work of men's hands... Human, and yet not wholly human, for the most heedless and the most cynical must see the finger of the divine...'

As before, racist ideas were used to justify the different standards of government applied abroad and in Britain. Lord Cromer, governor of Egypt, opined that 'free institutions in the full sense of the term must for generations to come be wholly unsuitable to countries such as India and Egypt... it will probably never be possible to make a Western silk purse out of an Eastern sow's ear'.

The fashionable philosophy of Social Darwinism – which involved the misapplication of Darwin's theory of evolution to the development of societies – was used to give a 'scientific' gloss to the scramble for colonies. 'The truth is,' wrote an observer in 1896, 'that what we call national rivalry is to all intents and purposes part of the universal scheme that makes Nature "red in tooth and claw"'.

The British, it was argued, should be bred and educated as a master race. Lord Rosebery wrote in 1900:

An Empire such as ours requires as its first condition an Imperial Race – a race vigorous and industrious and intrepid. Health of mind and body exalt a nation in the competition of the universe. The survival of the fittest is an absolute truth in the conditions of the modern world.

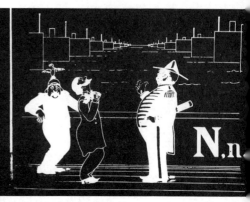

'THE WHITE MAN'S BURDEN'

At the same time, the British presented their appropriation of other people's countries as being done for altruistic or philanthropic reasons. Lord Curzon, viceroy of India, proclaimed: 'To me the message is carved in granite, hewn of the rock of doom: that our work is righteous and that it shall endure'. The British empire, he said, was 'under Providence, the greatest instrument for good that the world has seen'.[110]

In keeping with this mirage of British benevolence, colonised peoples everywhere were portrayed, as Sir Alfred Milner, Britain's top man in South Africa, said of the Africans, as 'children, needing and appreciating a just paternal government',[111] while nationalist movements were dismissed as irrelevant. English observers frequently claimed that the Irish were 'child-like'. Edith Balfour, who visited Ireland in 1905, wrote,

> They are like children listening to old fairy stories while their bread has to be earned...
>
> What would I not give... to help them? But the task is very difficult, and if you give children complete freedom they will certainly stray.[112]

The poet Rudyard Kipling, a leading apologist for empire, hated the Irish and supported the loyalist rebellion against Home Rule. He had nothing but foul-mouthed abuse for Ireland, calling it a 'dam' pernicious little bitch of a country' and classifying Irish nationalists with 'outbreaks of foot and mouth'.[113] It was Kipling who summed up for posterity the overbearing vanity of the British imperialists in his poem written in 1899:

Take up the White Man's burden –
Send forth the best ye breed –
Go bind your sons to exile
To serve your captives' need;
To wait in heavy harness
On fluttered folk and wild –
Your new-caught sullen peoples,
Half devil and half child.

Take up the White Man's burden –
The savage wars of peace –
Fill full the mouth of Famine
And bid the sickness cease;
And when your goal is nearest
The end for others sought,
Watch sloth and heathen Folly
Bring all your hope to naught.

66

I i   *Ii*

I is for India,
Our land in the East
Where everyone goes
To shoot tigers, and feast.

mperialist indoctrination began in the nursery, through books such as 'ABC for Baby Patriots' and 'Pictures for Little Englanders'

MEN of different trades and sizes
Here you see before your eyeses;
Lanky sword and stumpy pen,
Doing useful things for men;
When the Empire wants a stitch in her
Send for Kipling and for Kitchener.

The radical French artist Honoré Daumier opposed colonialism worldwide. In this
cartoon published in 1866 he attacked British repression in Ireland and Jamaica
– in 1865 Governor Eyre of Jamaica had responded to popular unrest by
unleashing a reign of terror. Here, as John Bull stands menacingly in the
background, a Jamaican whispers 'Patience' to an Irishman

RACISM IN THE SIX COUNTIES

While in Britain hostility was directed against the Irish in general, in Ireland it was 'Catholics' who were the target. Religion was the main feature distinguishing the settler population from the people they had dispossessed, and for centuries English governments had fostered the 'religious divide' in order to maintain control. In the late eighteenth century, Protestants and Catholics had come together to press for Irish independence, but Britain successfully used the 'divide and rule' tactic to undermine the movement.

The religious bigotry against Catholics which was a feature of British attitudes towards the Irish was even more virulently expressed by the ruling class within Ireland. In order to propagandise in support of their dominant position within Ireland, and the British link on which that depended, the 'Protestant Ascendancy' disguised their political aims in religious rhetoric. Thus in 1834, Irish Tories opposed Daniel O'Connell's Repeal movement with the words: 'Repeal is just a discreet word for Romish ascendancy and Protestant extermination.'[114]

In the 1890s, 'Home Rule is Rome Rule' became the battle cry of Ulster Unionists, and anti-clerical agitation reached formidable proportions. In 1898 George Bernard Shaw, who was himself from an Irish Protestant background, summed up the general attitude:

> Irish Protestantism was not then a religion: it was a side in a political faction, a class prejudice, a conviction that Roman Catholics are socially inferior persons who will go to Hell when they die and leave Heaven in the exclusive possession of Protestant ladies and gentlemen.[115]

In the second decade of the twentieth century, unionists rebelled violently against Home Rule, and were rewarded with a compromise: the partition of Ireland, with six counties in the northeast remaining under British rule, though with their own parliament at Stormont. The boundaries of the new statelet were drawn to ensure that the unionists had a two-thirds majority overall, but in large areas they were outnumbered by nationalists. In order to maintain control, and ensure that working class Protestants stayed loyal, the unionist upper classes turned the Six Counties into a police state, and institutionalised discrimination against Catholics, denying them equal access to votes, jobs, and housing.

In the early 1930s, Protestants and Catholics briefly united in demonstrations against unemployment. Unionist leaders promptly undermined the disaffection of Protestant workers by guaranteeing them a privileged position over Catholics. In July 1933, Sir Basil Brooke, a Stormont MP who later became prime minister of the North, was reported in the press as saying:

> There were a great number of Protestants and Orangemen who employed Roman Catholics. He felt he could speak freely on this subject as he had not a Roman Catholic about his own place... He would appeal to Loyalists therefore, wherever possible, to employ good Protestant lads and lassies.[116]

Then in April 1934 Stormont prime minister James Craig said: 'I have always said that I am an Orangeman first and a politician and a member of this parliament afterwards, all I boast is that we are a Protestant parliament for a Protestant state'.[117]

Inevitably, the apartheid-style regime was accompanied by apartheid-style ideas. The fundamentalists led by Ian Paisley – who won a majority of unionist votes at two successive European elections – portray their political campaign to keep the nationalist people in subjection as a religious crusade, and identify Catholicism with the Devil. As Paisley put it in his paper, the Protestant Telegraph, in 1967:

> Through Popery the Devil has shut up the way to our inheritance. Priestcraft, superstition and papalism with all their attendant vices of murder, theft, immorality, lust and incest, blocked the way to the land of gospel liberty.[118]

In a more recent taped sermon Paisley declaimed:

> We have a glorious Protestant heritage. It is great when one considers what it has delivered us from. From the chains, the tyranny, the ensnarement, the imprisonment of Romanism, with its priestcraft and idolatry. We have been brought from darkness to light, from bondage to freedom.[119]

Paisley has long-standing links with far-right religious institutions in the United States and has an honorary doctorate from the Bob Jones University of South Carolina, a racist institution which opposes the integration of blacks and whites.

Many Protestants perceive Catholics as inferior to themselves in social as well as religious terms. Though institutionalised discrimin-

Propaganda postcards from the loyalist campaign against Home Rule in 1912-14

INTRODUCTION CARD.

Class of placing

MINISTRY OF LABOUR, NORTHERN IRELAND.

IMPORTANT.

Refusal of suitable employment is a disqualification for the receipt of Unemployment Benefit

ALFRED STREET

Order No.......... Date............Class No........

......................ment Exchange Phone No..........

In the public interest, therefore, you are asked to state fully why you did not engage the applicant.

To.....................................

In reply to your request for......................

I am sending the bearer, M..........................

Please complete the space below and return this card to me as soon as possible, through the post, in the enclosed prepaid envelope.

Religion

......................193 **H. G. STEVENSON** *Manager.*

EMPLOYER'S REPLY.

Have you engaged the worker?...........

Date workhr is to start................

If the worker is not engaged please state overleaf the reason.

Please impress business stamp.

E.O. 18.

N. Ireland.

Signature.....................

Date..............195...

P.T.O.

C.i226 Wt.846 r3020 10,000 Gp.702 6/36 N.W.24.1
C.2036 Wt.1273 1154 10,000 Gp.161 1/36 N.W.146

ation was, and still is, responsible for the much higher Catholic unemployment rates, and for restricting Catholics largely to unskilled jobs, Protestants describe Catholics as lazy, work-shy and happy to live off state benefits. This stereotype is, of course, identical to that applied by racists to non-white people in Britain, and likewise conveniently justifies discrimination. David Calvert, a representative of Paisley's Democratic Unionist Party in the Northern Ireland Assembly, said in 1984:

> The Protestant people... want to get on in life, they work hard to achieve it, whereas there are very few Roman Catholic people who are prepared to take that line... It's often said that they're very keen on the half-crown but they're not very keen on the crown.[120]

A loyalist song put it this way:
and when their babies learn to talk
they shout 'discrimination'
their dad just lies in bed all day
and lives upon the nation.[121]

Again, in the typical racist tradition, some Protestants describe Catholics as dirty, drunken and stupid, and depict Catholic women as promiscuous. Needless to say, such Protestants flatter themselves that they are the polar opposite: hard-working, clean, sober and intelligent, with faithful and dutiful womenfolk.

'THE FINAL SOLUTION'

Some loyalists take the vilification of Catholics even further. A loyalist songbook published in 1974, for instance, referred to 'filthy rebel scum' and 'fenian swine'. A loyalist paper announced in 1971: 'The time will soon be ripe when the Republican scum will make their final effort... this time we must give them the final solution.' In May 1984 George Seawright, a representative of Paisley's Democratic Unionist Party in the Northern Ireland Assembly, caused a storm when he said the money spent on educating 'Fenian scum' would be better spent on buying incinerators and burning Catholics and their

priests. Seawright refused to withdraw his remarks, saying there would be 'no retraction, no apology, no compromise and no surrender.'[122]

This view of Catholics as an inferior and contemptible species leads logically to indiscriminate sectarian murder campaigns: several hundred Catholics have been murdered by Protestant paramilitaries for no other reason than that they were Catholics. Similarly in Britain, racist perceptions of black people have led to murders and countless assaults on people of Asian and West Indian origin, simply because of the colour of their skin.

Loyalists have even composed triumphalist songs to celebrate the killing of Catholics, who are often described by the derogatory term 'taigs'.[123] They exulted over the burning of Catholic houses in Bombay Street, Belfast, in 1969 with the words:

> On the 14th August we took a little trip
> Up along Bombay Street and burned out all the shit
> We took a little petrol and we took a little gun,
> And we fought the bloody Fenians, till we had them on the run.

Another song celebrated Bloody Sunday, 30 January 1972, when 14 unarmed demonstrators were shot dead by British troops:

> Sunday morning went for a drive,
> Took along my Colt 45.
> Hey, Hey, Hey, what a beautiful day.
> Went to Derry not on a hunch,
> Knew I'd get a taig before lunch,
> Hey, Hey, Hey, it's a beautiful day.

The chorus was:
> Bang, Bang, Bang, Bloody Sunday,
> This is my, my, my beautiful day.

Another loyalist ditty, also set to a popular tune, went:

> I was born under the Union Jack,
> I was born under the Union Jack,
> If Taigs are made for killing,
> Then blood is made to flow,
> You've never seen a place like Sandy Row.
>
> If guns are made for shooting,
> Then skulls are made to crack.
> You've never seen a better Taig
> Than with a bullet in his back.

Unsurprisingly, loyalist groups such as the legal paramilitary Ulster Defence Association and the illegal Ulster Volunteer Force have made common cause with fascist groups in Britain, such as the National Front, and have engaged in joint military training exercises.[124] In 1984 three loyalist teenagers who belonged to a group who called themselves 'NF SKINZ' were sentenced for killing a Catholic

The National Front marches through Coleraine in the North of Ireland in June 1984. Photo: Derek Spiers/Report

man in north Belfast.[125] The National Front has frequently attacked pro-Irish demonstrations in Britain, and has organised marches through towns in the Six Counties with the agreement of unionist councils. Loyalists have also long voiced support for regimes such as those in South Africa and pre-liberation Rhodesia. Further, Enoch Powell, one of Britain's most prominent racists, now has his political base in the Six Counties, representing the Official Unionist Party at Westminster from his seat in County Down.

For its part, the nationalist community has rarely responded to loyalist racism in kind. Though republican papers attack the politics of loyalism, they do not attack Protestant religious beliefs, nor do they employ racist stereotypes against Protestants. Rather, republicans recognise that loyalist racism is rooted in the maintenance of British rule in the Six Counties, and their hostility is primarily directed against the British state and its agents.

This lack of religious bigotry and racist thinking appears to be characteristic of anti-colonial movements the world over. Unlike nationalist movements in imperialist countries, nationalism in oppressed countries is more often expressed through pride in, and love for, the country in question, rather than in loathing of people perceived as 'alien'. As Professor Benedict Anderson has observed, 'Even in the case of colonised peoples, who have every reason to feel hatred for their imperialist rulers, it is astonishing how insignificant the element of hatred is in these expressions of national feeling.'[126]

IRELAND FORGOTTEN

After partition, and Britain's departure from 26 of Ireland's 32 counties in 1922, most people in Britain forgot about Ireland. The Six County parliament at Stormont was left to its own devices, and there was a convention at the House of Commons that the North's affairs were not discussed there. The media, following in the politicians' wake, likewise remained silent.

Partition left Ireland an anomaly in Western Europe. Then as now it was a white, Western country, in which English had largely supplanted the native language, but which at the same time shared certain characteristics with countries in the Third World: the Six Counties were politically and militarily occupied by Britain, with an armed police force and highly repressive laws; the South was underindustrialised and dependent on agriculture; it was economically dominated by Britain, and was in effect a neo-colony; and both parts of Ireland were subject to large-scale emigration. Ireland was also one of the very few western European countries that had not been involved in empire building, though it did export missionaries to the Third World.

Ireland's anomalous situation was reflected in the position of Irish immigrants in Britain. They continued to arrive to do heavy manual labour, domestic labour, factory work and nursing, but they were partially displaced from their position at the bottom of the hierarchy by other incoming people, more culturally or physically distinct: first the thousands of immigrants from eastern and central Europe, many

Cormac

74

of them Jewish, who began arriving towards the end of the nineteenth century, and then, after World War II, the people arriving from the West Indies, India and Pakistan.

These non-white immigrants became the scapegoats for the failures of the economy just as the Irish and Jews had been before them. During the 1960s and 1970s more people left Britain than arrived, and two-thirds of immigrants resident in 1971 were white. But immigration, and specifically black immigration, was defined by politicians and the media as 'the problem'. This notion was formalised in a series of racist immigration and nationality laws passed between 1962 and 1981. These laws virtually stopped immigration from black Commonwealth countries, while allowing white immigration – of 'patrials' from abroad, the Irish, and EEC nationals – to continue. Proclaiming in effect that non-white skin is unacceptable, these laws made racism the official policy of the British state.

But while the Irish were no longer the principal target of British racism, they were still economically and socially disadvantaged, and were still met by hostility and discrimination. In 1923 the town clerk of Helensburgh in Scotland was quoted as saying, 'An ordinary Irish population will reduce this new tenement to a slum in the course of a few years and therefore in this town Irish tenants are avoided as far as possible.'[127] 'No Irish, No Coloured, No Dogs' was an all too familiar feature of advertisements for lodgings in the 1950s. In 1966, Ealing Council successfully defeated a Race Relations Board prosecution, brought after an Irish person was refused housing, against its policy of housing only British or naturalised citizens. A study of children of immigrant groups in the 1970s concluded that what emerged quite clearly from surveys was 'the strikingly bad housing, employment and financial conditions in which the first-generation Asians and first- and second-generation West Indians and Irish 16 year-olds and their families live.'[128]

The old stereotypes of the Irish remained ingrained. The leading historian A.L. Rowse, for instance, continued the tradition of his predecessors. His book *The Expansion of Elizabethan England*, first published in 1955 to much acclaim, is peppered with comments which assume the existence of an inferior Celtic race: 'Murder never seems to have been rated very high in the Irish catalogue of crimes... Celts are still apt to be unwashed... time had rather stood still for Ireland, as it is apt to do for Celts...' In another passage, Rowse offered an interpretation in then-fashionable Freudian terms:

> For the Elizabethan Irish, Protestantism provided an ideology of active enterprise, forward-looking and dynamic. It is only just to admit that Catholicism not only better suited the nature of Irish society – such as we have seen it to be – but that it agreed with the backward-looking Celtic temperament, with its nostalgic urge to return to the womb, its refusal to come to terms with the facts of the external world, its deepest desire to withdraw into itself.[129]

The old prejudices about the Irish – and the British delusions of grandeur which accompanied them – continued to surface in a casual and unthinking way, as in this passage from a detective novel by Josephine Tey, published in 1948:

> She had turned to give him the tray to carry, and so was facing him with their hands almost touching. 'The Saxons have the two qualities that I value most in this world – two qualities that explain why they have inherited the earth: kindness and dependability, or tolerance and responsibility, if you prefer the terms. Two qualities the Celt never had; which is why the Irish have inherited nothing but squabbles. Oh, damn, I forgot the cream.'[130]

By 1967, when most British people were still unaware of the tensions building up in the North, and when black people were feeling the full force of British racism, the old hostility to the Irish lay just beneath the surface. A Gallup poll in October that year found that nearly a quarter of their sample thought that Irish immigration had had 'a harmful effect' on Britain.[131]

THE TROOPS GO IN

With the renewal of conflict in the North, and particularly the return of British soldiers to the streets in 1969, all the old prejudices erupted. Initially, British politicians and commentators sympathised with Catholic demands for civil rights and condemned the Unionist regime. But at the same time they behaved as if the bizarre and discriminatory system in the North had nothing to do with them,

In this Sunday Express cartoon, Cummings shows Ireland as Britain's problem – rather than the other way round. It was published on 15 August 1971, soon after the start of internment without trial

French cartoonist Patrik gives a different view

when in fact British patronage was the basic condition for its existence.

In August 1969, a concerted police attack on the nationalist Bogside area of Derry precipitated the entry of British troops. The people of the Bogside had beaten back the RUC, who were exhausted and demoralised, and the Northern Ireland government asked for troops to be sent in because, as the then Labour home secretary James Callaghan recalled: 'They feared that the centre of the city would then be invaded by a riotous mob with the prospect of looting, arson, injury to persons and extensive damage to property.'

But although, as Callaghan admitted, the troops were sent in to relieve the police and 'to prevent a breakdown of law and order', British people were told that the purpose of sending the troops was to bring peace to the warring Irish. Thus on 18 August 1969, four days after the troops intervened, the Daily Mirror printed a 'Historical Teach-In on Ireland' which told its readers that, 'The Irish agree on one thing only. That is to go on arguing and fighting about a peace that has not existed in their history.'[133]

Immediately after a Conservative government took power in June 1970, the British army launched all-out attacks on nationalist areas and it became abundantly clear that the British government was more interested in preserving the status quo than in reform. The IRA, which had been dormant in 1969, became stronger and more active, killing the first British soldier in early 1971. Whenever the British government appeared to be making conciliatory moves towards the nationalists, loyalist paramilitaries – who had killed innocent Catholics as far back as 1966, and had killed the first policeman in 1969 – began random sectarian assassination campaigns.

Over succeeding years, the British authorities, aided by the media, presented a topsy-turvy picture of events in order to sustain the image of British impartiality. They played down the atrocities committed by the British forces, minimised loyalist responsibility for violence, and depicted the situation as one long succession of violent acts committed by republicans. They portrayed the IRA as the cause – rather than a product – of the conflict, and did their utmost to exclude nationalist political views from the media. They refused to acknowledge that partition and the continuing British presence were the root of the problem, and denounced those who questioned Britain's role as 'traitors'.

It was the same old story. The British authorities presented themselves – as they still do – as disinterested and above the fray, intervening between 'warring factions' to 'prevent a bloodbath'. In 1983, for instance, the Sunday Times proclaimed that 'Since 1969... the main note of British policy in Northern Ireland has been altruism.'[134] The Irish, on the other hand, were depicted as irrationally violent, indulging in what journalist Milton Schulman described as 'the senseless pastime of murdering each other',[135] and in need of a firm guiding hand. In 1977, when the RUC were using torture to obtain confessions, the Sunday Times summed up the prevailing attitude, pro-

nouncing that 'The notorious problem is how a civilised country can overpower uncivilised people without becoming less civilised in the process.'[136]

The same view permeates the history text books that are used in English schools. Ireland rarely enters the curriculum even in schools with a large number of children of Irish descent: when it does, as researcher Mary Hickman has demonstrated, the Irish are generally shown as 'the problem' and the British as 'the problem solvers'.[137] Thus R.J. Cootes, in a book titled *Britain Since 1700* and published in 1972 by Longman, wrote: 'In 1969 bitter fighting broke out in the streets of Belfast and other northern towns. British troops were sent in to keep the peace, but longstanding religious differences could not be settled overnight.' Another text, published in 1976, described the British army as having 'the thankless task of trying to preserve some semblance of peace and order in a society where violence and terrorism have often led to retaliation.'[138]

The racism inherent in this view of 'civilised' Britain intervening to sort out the 'uncivilised' Irish on occasion comes blatantly into the open. In an article written immediately before the death of Bobby Sands MP on hunger strike, right-wing journalist Peregrine Worsthorne defended Britain against international criticism with these words:

> The English have every reason to feel proud of their country's recent record in Northern Ireland, since it sets the whole world a uniquely impressive example of altruistic service in the cause of peace. Nothing done by any other country in modern times so richly deserves the Nobel prize...
> This, I think, is where the IRA makes its greatest mistake: in underestimating the maturity of the British people, their unique capacity to carry on without the kind of sentimental uplift which less adult breeds find so essential for sustained resolve and sacrifice.[139]

CRUDE PREJUDICE

In this climate of ignorant self-congratulation, it is scarcely surprising that crude anti-Irish prejudice has flourished. Just as in previous centuries, the Irish are regularly depicted in the press and on television as stupid, drunken and backward. Thus in 1977 *Times* columnist Bernard Levin invoked the Victorian stereotype to denigrate Irish people who support the reunification of Ireland: 'There they go still, the Irish 'pathriots' [sic], with minds locked and barred, mouths gaping wide to extrude the very last morsel of folly, and consumed with a wild terror at the prospect that sense may one day prevail.'[140]

In 1982, when Gerry Adams, Danny Morrison and Martin McGuinness of Sinn Féin, newly elected members of the Northern Ireland Assembly, were banned from entering Britain, Levin wrote an account of an imaginary conversation between them and Labour members of the Greater London Council, who had invited them

" Mr. Pym, tell President Galtieri if he wished to claim sovereignty over the island of Ireland, we'd back him to the hilt "

over.[141] Levin's piece, which must rank among the most vicious ever written and which led to numerous protests, depicted the GLC members as jargon-spouting leftists and the Sinn Fein representatives as inarticulate, racist drunks.

Another right-wing journalist fond of abusing the Irish is Auberon Waugh. Commenting on Ireland's neutrality in the Falklands/Malvinas war in 1982, he wrote in the Sunday Telegraph: 'It is tempting to yearn for a return of the Vikings to plunder Ireland's coastal areas and rape her nuns so that we, too, can have an opportunity to declare high-minded neutrality and demand a diplomatic solution.'[142] And in January 1984 John Junor, the editor of the Sunday Express, had this to say about US President Reagan's proposed vote-catching trip to Ireland: 'Ah well, every man to his own taste. For my own part, I would infinitely prefer to spend three days in June looking for worms in a dung heap.'[143]

Even elevated cultural figures are not above denigrating the Irish. The well-known television dramatist Dennis Potter, for instance, reminisced in the Sunday Times[144] in December 1983 about an encounter during the making of a film:

'I swear to God you must be Irish,' reiterated the huge and amiable Irish-American actor Brian Dennehey, mistaking occasional rhetoric and fre-

an Ancient Irish joke

quent booze for the bloodline of his own miserable tribe. I simply could not make him understand that he was insulting me.

WHEN ARE IRISH PEOPLE BRITISH?

In keeping with this disparagement of the Irish, British pundits have developed what an Irish Times writer described as 'the tedious English habit of claiming any notable Irish achievements as British'.[145] This tendency was remarked on at the start of the century by George Bernard Shaw, who wrote that the historian Macaulay, 'seeing that the Irish had in Swift an author worth stealing, tried to annex him by contending that he must be classed as an Englishman because he was not an aboriginal Celt.' Shaw commented sarcastically that Macaulay 'might as well have refused the name of Briton to Addison because he did not stain himself blue and attach scythes to the poles of his sedan chair.'[146]

In 1983 the Irish poet Seamus Heaney was so annoyed at finding himself included in the *Penguin Book of Contemporary British Verse* – he had thought the book would be titled *Open Ground* – that he wrote a 33-verse poem[147] to emphasise that he is not British but Irish:

As empire rings its curtain down
   This "British" word
Sticks deep in native and *colon*
   Like Arthur's sword.

…don't be surprised
If I demur, for, be advised
   My passport's green
No glass of ours was ever raised
   To toast *The Queen*.

Similarly, as letters to the Irish Post have pointed out, when Irish people do something courageous – as when an Irishman rescued two people from a blazing car in North London in 1982 – reports in the press do not mention their nationality. Yet when an Irish person is sent to prison for even a minor misdemeanour, the word 'Irish' often features in the headline.

Phil Evans

81

From the Daily Express, 12 August 1970

"How marvellous it would be if they DID knock each other insensible!"

CARTOONS

Some of the most vicious attacks on the Irish have come from cartoonists, particularly those working for 'popular' newspapers. In line with the requirements of their job, cartoonists have reflected and exaggerated the main themes of the press coverage. With rare exceptions, they have presented British politicians and soldiers as long-suffering 'peace-keepers', caught up in a war not of their own making between violent and irrational Irish people.

By mid-1970, when British troops went on the offensive against the nationalist community, cartoonists had reverted to Victorian images of the Irish, depicting them as primitive and ape-like in contrast to the more refined-looking squaddies. This view of the Irish has remained a

Below left: From the Daily Express, 11 August 1971, two days after the start of internment without trial. Below right: An Irish view of the British army from Óisín, cartoonist of Andersonstown News, based in nationalist west Belfast

"I'm the last surviving Irishman—but not for long—my left hand won't allow my right hand to have the last word in the argument."

THE PROFESSIONALS

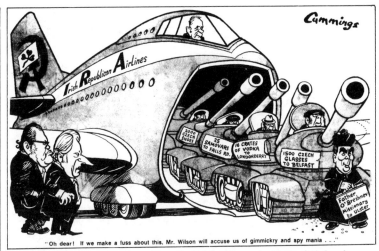

"Oh dear! If we make a fuss about this, Mr. Wilson will accuse us of gimmickry and spy mania . . ."

constant theme. Questioned by the Irish Times in 1982, Michael Cummings, who draws for the Express, said he claimed cartoonist's licence for giving expression to the biased British view that the Irish were 'extremely violent, bloodyminded, always fighting, drinking enormous amounts, getting roaring drunk.' The IRA's violence, he said, tended to 'make them look rather like apes – though that's rather hard luck on the apes.' He went on:

> There is a rather curious convention, too – the Irish tend as a nation to have rather long upper lips. The cartoonist Jak [of the Standard] had all his Irish people with sideburns to the middle of their cheeks, that was his way of putting over the Irish.

He added, referring to his own work: 'One shows people looking sour if they are making antipathetic remarks about you – though one wouldn't show a perfectly charming man like Garret Fitzgerald like that.'[148]

One cartoon by Cummings provoked strong protests from workers at the Scottish Daily Express in Glasgow in 1971. The cartoon showed an aeroplane, marked 'Irish Republican Airlines', disgorging a fleet of tanks with labels such as '25 samovars to Falls Road'. Ahead of the tanks was Russian leader Brezhnev, dressed as a priest, holding a case marked 'Father O'Brezhnev, missionary to Ulster'.[149]

Some of the Express workers were Catholic and of Irish extraction, and they felt that the cartoon was offensive and a libel on innocent Catholics. They also feared that the cartoon would have an inflammatory effect on relations between Glasgow's Catholic and Protestant communities. After arguments with the paper's editor and deputy editor, nine engineers and electricians went home, bringing production to a standstill, and 351,000 copies of the paper were lost. The paper's editors in Manchester, however, where the Irish edition was printed, took a different line from the Glasgow editors: they simply decided not to carry the cartoon.

THE JAK CARTOON

The cartoon that generated the biggest storm to date was a drawing by Jak carried in London's evening paper, the Standard, on 29 October 1982. It showed a man walking past a cinema poster advertising a film called 'THE IRISH', which was billed as 'THE ULTIMATE IN PSYCHOPATHIC HORROR'. The poster was illustrated with grotesque figures wielding an array of gruesome weapons in a graveyard.

As the Standard later admitted, many people were angered by the cartoon. The Irish in Britain Representation Group raised their objections with the Ethnic Minorities Unit of the Greater London Council. A full meeting of the GLC later decided to ban advertising, worth some £100,000 per year, in the Standard. GLC leader Ken Livingstone said:

> The clear message of the cartoon is that the Irish, as a race and as a community, are murderous, mindless thugs... I do not believe in free speech for racists... We will not put another penny into the Standard while they continue to vilify the Irish.[150]

The Standard remained unrepentant, saying that the situation in 'Ulster' 'does make the average American horror movie look positively anodyne.'

The Commission for Racial Equality asked the Attorney-General to prosecute the Standard, and also complained to the Press Council. But the Commission later withdrew the complaints, saying that a prosecution under the Race Relations Act would not have succeeded, and that the Standard had given a 'satisfactory' justification. Despite the fact that the 'film' depicted in the cartoon was titled 'The Irish', the Standard claimed that the cartoon was not 'aimed at innocent Irish people'.

The Press Council proved useless. It not only rejected the complaints brought by the GLC and an Irish reader of the Standard, but went further, upholding a complaint from the Standard and ruling that the GLC's action 'was a blatant attempt by a local authority to use the power of its purse to influence the contents of a newspaper article and coerce the editor.' The GLC, however, remained firm. Ken Livingstone condemned the Press Council as 'an appalling Tory body', and said it remained GLC policy to withhold advertising until the Standard made a full apology for its offensive cartoon.

Within weeks of the Press Council's decision, similar events in New Zealand came to a very different conclusion. Shortly after the IRA bombed soldiers in London in July 1982, the New Zealand Truth, a racy tabloid weekly, published an editorial which concluded:

> While terrorism in any form, in any country, is appalling, there is something about the Irish brand – like that of the PLO against Israel – that makes Irish (or Palestinian) nationality difficult to bear among civilised people.[151]

The Irish ambassador, Joseph Small, complained to prime minister Robert Muldoon, who suggested he take the issue to the New

Cartoonist Jak of London's Standard uses the same derogatory stereotype for the Irish and trade unionists

Zealand Press Council and to the Race Relations Conciliator. In April 1983, the Press Council found that the editorial had exceeded the bounds of reasonable comment. The Race Relations Conciliator, Hiwi Tauroa, a Maori, found that the editorial was in breach of a section of the New Zealand Race Relations Act which states:

> It shall be unlawful for any person to publish or distribute written matter which is threatening, abusive, or insulting, being matter or words likely to excite hostility or ill-will against, or bring into contempt or ridicule, any group of persons in New Zealand on the ground or the colour, race, or ethnic or national origins of that group of persons.

There is a similar section in the British Public Order Act. The editor of the Truth said his newspaper regretted the breach of the Act, and apologised to the ambassador and people of Irish descent in New Zealand.

British establishment attitudes have changed little. In this turn-of-the-century cartoon, 'ungrateful Paddy' is portrayed as the only member of the imperial family not satisfied with the blessings of British civilisation

ANTI-IRISH JOKES

In a situation where the Irish are constantly denigrated, and where the war in the North is blamed on Irish 'irrationality' rather than British policy, it is scarcely surprising that the centuries-old anti-Irish joke has flourished once again.

In 1971 a survey of the popular television show, *The Comedians*, revealed that jokes against the Irish were the second most frequent in the repertoire, with jokes against Pakistanis heading the list. During the seventies, books of anti-Irish jokes, sold on station bookstalls and in other popular outlets, achieved astonishing sales. Between 1977 and 1979 the publishing house Futura sold 485,000 copies of three 'Official Irish Joke' books.[152]

Anti-Irish jokes hinge on the notion that the Irish are stupid. They are often sexist as well as racist. Many Irish people were outraged when a snooker player in a television competition told 'the one about the Irish rapist who tied his victim's legs together so that she could not run away.'

Along with the 'jokes', a trade has developed in anti-Irish novelty goods: among them the 'Irish rubik cube', coloured green all over, on which none of the squares move and bearing the logo, 'One million sold – to the inventor'; the 'Irish' computer disk, which consists of a notepad and pencil; and the ubiquitous poster titled 'A LETTER FROM AN IRISH MOTHER', which begins:

> Dear Son,
>   Just a few lines to let you know I'm still alive. I'm writing this letter slowly because I know you can't read fast. You won't know the house when you get home – we have moved.

And so on. This 'letter' has been in circulation for a very long time. A Sheffield University researcher unearthed 49 versions of it: the earliest was dated 1795 and began, 'I have sent you nine shillings by the Chester Carrier; the carriage of which comes only to a guinea.'[153]

Complaints about the sale of such items have sometimes been successful. In 1976 Tony Corinda of K.B. Cards Limited of London was persuaded to withdraw from some shops a card for 'Members of the Irish Intelligence Club', which showed the bearer's IQ as 001½ and the date of issue as 31 February. Corinda acted reluctantly: 'we were selling hundreds of them,' he said. In 1982 after a complaint from writer Dónall Mac Amhlaigh a Nottinghamshire Co-op withdrew a T-shirt which carried the slogan: 'If you want your own dope, plant a Paddy'. The same year, the Woolworth's chain withdrew anti-Irish joke books and posters from all its outlets after the Irish in Britain Representation Group had picketed some of its north London stores.

On other occasions, such complaints have not produced results, probably because of the profits made on such goods: the Reject Pot Shop in London's Camden Town sold more than 600 'genuine Irish mugs' – emblazoned with shamrocks and with the handle inside – over two years. The General Store in London's fashionable Covent Garden withdrew the same mugs for a short time in 1982, saying that they might have been considered inflammatory in the wake of IRA bombings in London; they later put them back on sale and claimed they were selling better than ever because of the publicity. The Attorney General, Sir Michael Havers, refused a request from the Irish in Britain Representation Group that he prosecute shops selling these mugs.

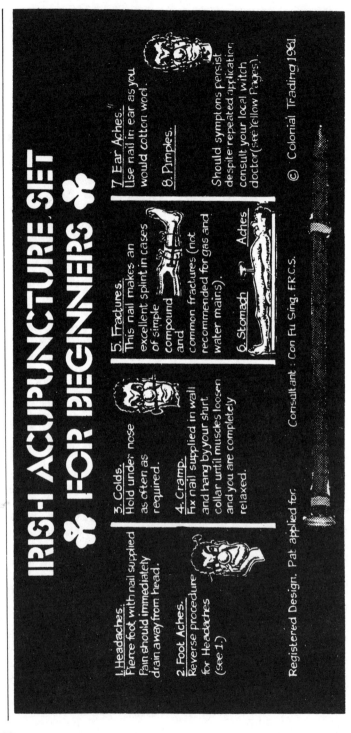

An example of the anti-Irish novelty goods widely sold in English gift shops: this 'acupuncture set' consists of a card with a six-inch nail attached

FUNNY OR RACIST?

When people complain about anti-Irish jokes and novelties, they are often accused of lacking a sense of humour. 'Everyone should be able to laugh at themselves,' they are told. But how often do we hear English people telling, or laughing at, jokes about the stupid English? In fact, few such jokes circulate in England – though anti-Pom jokes are told in Australia, and jokes about stupid British army intelligence officers are sometimes told in the North of Ireland – since Irish people, and other 'ethnic minorities', have not tended to respond to racism with racism. But Irish people do tell some jokes which poke fun at the English sense of superiority:

> Heard the one about the two Englishmen who were trying to have a go at an Irishman in a pub? One of them goes up to the Irishman and says, 'Did you know the Pope's a bastard?' The Irish man takes no notice. Then the other Englishman goes up to him and says, 'Hey, Paddy! Did you know the Pope's an Englishman?' 'Yes, I know,' says the Irishman. 'Your mate's just told me.'

The leading Cambridge anthropologist Edmund Leach examined several best-selling anti-Irish joke books for an article in the magazine New Society.[154] He pointed out that jokes are 'culture-bound': what is funny to one society or group may be unfunny or meaningless to another group. Having looked in detail at the anti-Irish jokes, he concluded that the 'prototype of the stage Irishman' who emerged from them

> is not so much a figure of fun as an object of contempt merging into deep hostility. He is a drink-addicted moron, reared in the bog, who wears his rubber boots at all times, cannot read or write, and constantly reverses the logic of ordinary common sense. His female counterpart shares the same qualities, except that she is sexually promiscuous, rather than perpetually drunk:

Humour is seldom 'just a joke'. These 'funny' postcards were used to attack the suffragettes

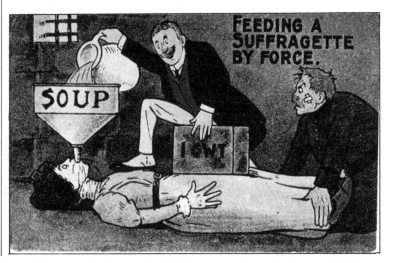

FEEDING A SUFFRAGETTE BY FORCE.

SOUP

89

No laughing matter!

Some British national newspapers recently carried the story about the Englishman who went on holiday to Yugoslavia and took lots of photographs. But when he returned home and had the photographs developed, he discovered that, instead of picturesque views of mountains and beaches, he had taken 24 perfect pictures of his right ear. The reason was that he had held the camera the wrong way around.

He was quoted as saying: "It must have been an Irish camera".

This is a perfect illustration of the intellectual content of the 'Irish' joke and of the intelligence of those who make them up.

MALACHY HEAVEY
Aldershot,
Hants.

■ The Scottish Sunday Post has just published the following 'Irish' joke:

"An Ayrshire man, fiddling with his car radio, picked up the Irish station, Radio Eireann. At noon, the programme switched to a recording clock striking the hour. But did it stop at 12? It went on ringing — 13, 14, 15, 16. Must be the new fangled 24-hour clock!"

The fact is that Radio Eireann has never used a recording clock striking the hour. What the Ayrshire man heard on RTE was the Angelus.

PETER BUTTERLY

Laughing

There was an anti - Irish joke in a recent episode 'Coronation Street'. I am told that it was a contri inclusion, which had nothing at all to do with storyline. Mike O'Hara, who lives in Belvedere, Ke wrote complaining to Granada Television who prode the series. He received a reply from the compan programme controller, Mike Scott. The following is main part of his reply:

"I suspect there are jokes not just about the Irish about many other stereotypes in the programme, and am quite certain that the jokes you complain about we not in any way intended to be racist. Thinking of anoth series of ours, 'The Comedians', where there was a mo sustained flow of jokes, I can remember English, Iris Jewish and coloured jokes galore which, far from bei attacks on the people concerned, were really in the gre tradition of British comedians in that over the year rather than aggravate racist situations, they defuse them".

To that letter, Mike O'Hara replied. The following an extract:

"Unfortunately the term 'Irish joke' has become euphemism for insult and a comfortable way of makin racist remarks in the thin guise of humour — racist made easy. It is a long time since I heard an Irish jok that was actually funny and when one does pop up it i enjoyed by nobody more than the Irish themselves.,,

"Your letter, if I may say so, also illustrates what is possibl the most disappointing aspect of the matter, which is tha perfectly decent people are quite happy to hear a flood of anti Irish remarks and pass them off as 'harmless'. Complacenc and/or indifference are the staunch allies of racism, as histor amply demonstrates.

"As an exercise, on hearing an 'Irish' joke or remark broad cast or in conversation, substitute the word 'English' and see whether you would not soon find it offensive.

"Certain publications which rightly condemn the activities of organisation avail themselves of every opportunity

'O'Reilly does other things besides drink' – 'Like what?' – 'Well, he hiccups.'

The humour in the jokes, said Leach, is 'grade z'. So why do such large numbers of people buy the books? He suggested an answer to this question by comparing anti-Irish jokes to the jokes told within – not against – the Jewish community:

Jokes about Jews are told by Jews to other Jews. They are an expression of international Jewish cultural solidarity, and they are often very clever. 'Irish' jokes are, in every respect, just the reverse. The sheer stupidity of both the joke and the characters described flatters the reader into a belief that there are others, who are not like me, who may be intellectually even more limited than myself. The ethnic element in 'Irish' jokes is thus latently racist. It would make no sense at all to substitute 'Jew' for 'Irishman'. But 'West Indian' or 'Pakistani' is different.

Propaganda not a joke

Britain has long been a capitalist and imperialist county. Its rulers have always had a vested interest in trying to: (a) justify their plunder and oppression in Ireland; and (b) divide and rule the workers of different nationalities in Britain.

It is well documented that on successive occasions when the Irish people sought to resist British rule, the anti-Irish joke emerged in Britain.

The Irish were cast as drunkards and simple minded and that they loved fighting for the sheer joy of it. One has only to look at the files of 'Punch' to find proof for all of this.

This 'humour' always served the purpose of confusing the ordinary public in Britain and preventing them from appreciating that the Irish have a just cause.

The current bout of joke propaganda concentrates on the Irishman as a 'thick'. The jokes began with the emergence of the Northern Ireland situation in 1969 and received their biggest promotion on the 'Comedians' television series. As always in the past, the jokes help the British Government's line on Northern Ireland — sustaining the story that the war there is a religious one between people who are 'thick' and who haven't any logical reason for behaving as they do.

The troops are presented as heroically keeping the peace.

In addition, the relegation of the Irish to the limbo of the sub-intelligent and, therefore, sub-human is a device which justifies anything and everything that is done to us. As well, being sub-human our opinions can't really count or be logical.

So when people take a stand against these jokes, I applaud. I particularly congratulate the Irish community in Kidderminster for their stand, as you reported in your issue of July 23. The students involved who repudiated the jokes are also to be congratulated.

These jokes are not harmless — nor are they intended to be. Every Irish person should take a stand against them and patiently explain their significance to the ordinary decent working British people — some of whom don't approve of these sick jokes anyway.

As for those Irish comedians who help propagate these jokes, we should isolate them completely.

**DIARMUID BREANACH
London SE9.**

Many Irish people living in Britain find anti-Irish jokes deeply offensive. The Irish Post, paper of the Irish in Britain, often publishes their protests. Above, from left to right: From the Irish Post, 17 October 1981, 11 April 1981, 27 August 1977.

Jokes identical in theme – and often in content – to anti-Irish jokes are told by Americans against Poles, by Glaswegians against 'teuchters' – country bumpkins, and by Irish people against the countryfolk of Kerry. In each case, the group who tell the jokes are asserting their superiority and bolstering their own sense of self-importance. A Polish-American journalist who spoke out against the anti-Polish jokes told in the States – such as 'a Polish dictionary is full of blank pages', and 'a Polish pencil has an eraser at both ends' – said: 'Those so-called jokes are meant to demean the victim while giving the impression that the teller is a very bright and superior person indeed.'[155]

Similarly, jokes told against black people and jokes told against women allow whites and men to congratulate themselves in the mistaken belief that they are 'superior', and justify their dominance over the other group.

COLD CALCULATION

That such humour is far from being 'harmless fun' is demonstrated by the calculating way in which it has been used by the Sun newspaper, which is blatantly right-wing and the most widely read of British dailies, with an estimated readership of over 12 million.

During the Falklands/Malvinas war of 1982, the Sun – which cheered the sinking of the Argentinian ship, the General Belgrano, with the loss of hundreds of lives, with the headline 'GOTCHA!' – instituted a daily series of 'Argy-bargie' jokes, offering £5 for every reader's joke published. Similarly, when French farmers were protesting in early 1984 against the importation of cheap meat from Britain, the Sun launched a 'Hop off you frogs' campaign. The level of awareness of some Sun readers was indicated by a survey, quoted by an Open University lecturer in 1982, which revealed that one-third of Sun readers polled believed it was a Labour paper.[156]

The Sun and other 'pop' papers have responded viciously to attempts to challenge anti-Irish humour. In December 1982, when Islington Council passed a resolution condemning anti-Irish jokes – and also opposing the use of plastic bullets and the British presence in the North of Ireland – the Sun responded with an editorial headed 'What a laugh'. Despite the fact that only months before, during the Falklands/Malvinas war, the Sun had launched a campaign calling for a boycott of all things pertaining to the 'contemptible, treacherous Irish', the paper now remarked that 'the would-be dictators of Islington's Marxist Council... are so dead from the neck up that they cannot understand that the jokes spring from affection.'[157]

It was the same story the following year, when the Irish in Islington Project was set up with funds from the Greater London Council. The Project was allocated two full-time workers, each paid £8,600 per year, committed to a wide range of welfare and cultural tasks. For an

In this doubly racist cartoon from the Daily Express of 12 September 1969, Cummings uses a derogatory stereotype of 'primitive' black people to emphasise the 'animal' behaviour of the Irish

"We're pagan missionaries come to try to make peace among the bloodthirsty Christians"

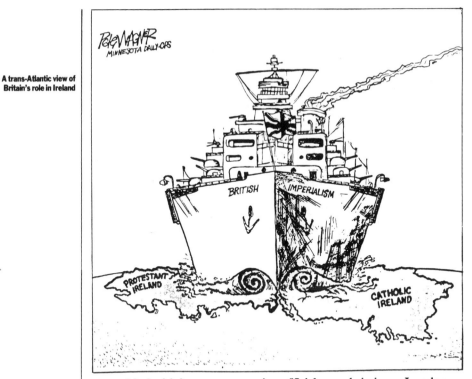

area with the highest concentration of Irish people in inner London, the grant was not large.

The 'pop' press responded to this initiative with a barrage of hostility and lies. Some reports said, wrongly, that Islington had funded the project. All focussed on – and ridiculed – just one of the

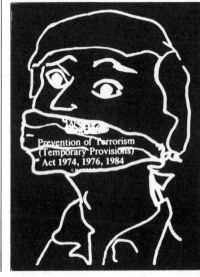

The Prevention of Terrorism Act has been extensively used to harass Irish people living in Britain and deter them from political activity. The PTA allows for people to be detained without charge for up to seven days, and for the Home Secretary to exclude people, including UK citizens born in Northern Ireland, from Britain without trial or explanation. The PTA was first passed in 1974, then replaced by a new Act in 1976, which in turn was replaced in 1984. The latest PTA covers not only Irish but also international political activity.

Between November 1974 and 26 March 1984, 5,802 people were detained in Britain under the PTA. The vast majority of these, 5,083, were released without charge. A further 274 were excluded from Britain. Only 7.6% (444) of those detained were charged with any offence (two thirds of them were charged under Acts other than the PTA), and only 5.7% (331) were found guilty of any offence. Thus 94.3% of those detained were innocent of any offence.

Project's aims, described in its manifesto as 'to combat anti-Irish racism in the media'. 'Heard the one about the £17,000 Irish "joke"?' cried London's Standard. 'GAG THE MICKEY TAKERS – £17,000 jobs to stop Irish jokes', raged the Daily Star. '£17,000 TO SAVE IRISH!', laughed the Sun. 'Pay-off for Irish jokes', announced the Daily Mirror, while the Sunday People proclaimed that 'The left-wing council of a London borough has gone to the loony limit.'[158]

As Islington chief whip Alan Clinton pointed out, the press response was itself 'a blatant example' of the anti-Irish racism which the Project aimed to oppose.

THE GARBAGE OF WIT

As Maria Edgeworth and her father pointed out in their *Essay on Irish Bulls* published in 1802, the type of humour which hinges on the stupidity of others has been around a long time and in all sorts of places: 'Many bulls, reputed to be born and bred in Ireland, are of foreign extraction; and many more, supposed to be unrivalled in their kind, may be matched in all their capital points.'[159] The Edgeworths discovered examples of anecdotes that had resurfaced as 'Irish' from not only other European countries, such as France and Spain, but also ancient Greece!

The Edgeworths gave a scathing view of the kind of people who tell such jokes, writing:

> there are people who justify the assertion, that laughter always arises from a sense of real or imaginary superiority. Now if it be true, that laughter has its source in vanity, as the most ignorant are generally the most vain, they must enjoy this pleasure in its highest perfection. Unconscious of their own deficiencies, and consequently fearless of becoming in their turn the objects of ridicule, they enjoy in full security the delight of humbling their superiors... Wise men may be struck with admiration, respect, doubt or humility; but the ignorant, happily unconscious that they know nothing, can be checked in their merriment by no consideration, human or divine. No fastidious delicacy spoils their sports of fancy; though ten times told, the tale to them never can be tedious; though dull 'as the fat weed that grows on Lethe's bank,' the jest for them has all the poignancy of satire: of the very offals, the garbage of wit, they can feed and batten.

It could be said that jokes about the stupidity of others are international jokes in search of a subject. Different groups of people attach the jokes to different subjects – but what all the subjects have in common is that they are resented in some way by the tellers, or perceived as inferior. The Irish, dominated, exploited and impoverished by Britain for centuries, were an obvious choice as the subject for such jokes.

In turn, the telling of anti-Irish jokes has created in the minds of many English people an instantaneous association between Irish nationality and stupidity. It has reinforced and made socially acceptable chauvinist attitudes to the Irish and their political objectives. It has helped to create a climate in which few ask questions when soldiers or policemen torture people or kill children with plastic bullets. It represents a propaganda 'plus' for the government, and eases its task of justifying Britain's continuing presence in the North, and the injustice that entails.

THE BUTCHER'S APRON

Today, under Queen Elizabeth II, Britain remains in Ireland for the same reason that four centuries ago Queen Elizabeth I despatched troops and colonists there: not altruism, but expediency, to secure 'Britain's west flank'.

Britain's presence in the North of Ireland cannot be justified as 'democratic', since Ireland was partitioned against the wishes of its people. Nor does Britain remain there out of support to 'kith and kin'; loyalists are dismissed as 'Paddies' just like all other Irish people, and, as a secret government report of 1949 revealed, even if loyalists wanted Britain out, Britain might not agree, because of the 'first-class strategic importance' of the North.

The continuation of British rule over the North of Ireland has meant the maintenance of what is, to all intents and purposes, a police state. More than a third of the community is subjected to systematic discrimination and repression, to which violence is the inevitable response.

But English people have been encouraged – by unscrupulous politicians, by servile television companies and newspapers, by tame historians and unquestioning teachers – to remain cocooned in complacent ignorance about Britain's role in the North. The regeneration of ancient prejudices towards the Irish has been one result.

The problem of English racism – whether against the Irish or against black people – is not just a question of many English people having mistaken ideas about other people. It is also a question of the mistaken view that many English people hold of themselves, of Britain's history and of Britain's role in the world today.

Irish perspectives from Cormac of An Phoblacht/Republican News

An RUC man fires a fatal plastic bullet at John Downes on 12 August 1984. He was the fifteenth person to be killed by this weapon in the North of Ireland. Anti-Irish racism desensitises British people to atrocities committed in their name.

There is a fundamental paradox. Britain has one of the most violent and uncivilised histories of any European country, yet the orthodox view is that the English are both non-violent and civilised, and that it is the people whom Britain has oppressed who are violent and uncivilised.

A gigantic exercise in self-delusion has helped to preserve English pride and self-regard down the centuries. Actions taken for reasons of political and economic expediency have been presented as if altruism were the sole motive. Atrocities of all kinds – from Cromwell's massacre at Drogheda, to the slave-trade, to the appropriation of vast tracts of other people's countries – have been justified by claims of religious, cultural and racial superiority. As a result, many English people are unable to see themselves as others see them: to recognise why in other parts of the world the Union Jack has been described as the 'butcher's apron', and the empire as 'the place where the sun never sets and the blood never dries'.

The time is long overdue for many English people to take a long, hard look at their own history, and at Britain's role in Ireland and other parts of the world today. It is time to recognise that the notion

that the English have always been a homogeneous nation of white Anglo-Saxon Protestants is a myth; that the notion that the language, culture and history of the British ruling class are more admirable than those of other people is a myth; that the notion that the British empire was 'great', or was established for reasons other than profit and self-interest, is a myth; that the notion that British people or white people are in any way superior to anyone else is a myth; and that the notion that Britain's conduct in the North of Ireland is democratic or altruistic is a myth.

These myths have served the British ruling class well over the centuries, clouding the harsh reality of exploitation and colonisation. Today, these myths help them to maintain their unjust occupation of part of Ireland, to use black English people as scapegoats for the failures of the system, and to amass great wealth at the expense of the peoples of the Third World. These myths must be challenged and destroyed if we are to achieve freedom and justice for Ireland, and build England, Scotland and Wales into just societies, no longer dependent on the exploitation of people either within or outside their borders, and with social and economic equality for all.

A a - / a

A is the Army
That dies for the Queen:
Its the very best Army
That ever was seen.

A.a.

Verses and drawings from ABC
for Baby Patriots

The crest of Sir John Hawkins,
who led the first English slave-
raiding expedition in 1562

REFERENCES

1. Richard Lovell Edgeworth and Maria Edgeworth, *Essay on Irish Bulls*, London, 4th edition 1815.
2. *Irish Post*, 14 April 1984.
3. Joan Inglis, 'The Irish in Britain: a question of identity', *Irish Studies in Britain*, no. 3, Spring/Summer 1982.
4. A.L. Morton, *A People's History of England*, Berlin: Seven Seas 1938, 1965, pp. 68-9.
5. Robert Bartlett, *Gerald of Wales 1146-1223*, Oxford: Clarendon Press 1982, p. 14.
6. Article by Kathleen Hughes in ed. Brian de Breffny, *The Irish World*, London: Thames and Hudson 1977, p. 68.
7. Peter Berresford Ellis, *A History of the Irish Working Class*, London: Gollancz 1972, p. 28.
8. Article by Roger Stalley in ed. Brian de Breffny, *The Irish World*, London: Thames and Hudson 1977, p. 82.
9. Robert Bartlett, *op.cit.*, pp. 169-70.
10. Gerald of Wales, *The History and Topography of Ireland*, Penguin Classics 1982.
11. Robert Bartlett, *op. cit.*, p. 13.
12. Ned Lebow, 'British historians and Irish history', *Eire-Ireland*, vol. VIII, no. 4, Winter 1973, p.12.
13. Introduction to Gerald of Wales, *The History and Topography of Ireland*, Penguin Classics 1982, p. 13.
14. W.R. Jones, 'England against the Celtic fringe: a study in cultural stereotypes', *Journal of World History*, xiii, 1 (1971), p. 159.
15. A.L. Rowse, *The Expansion of Elizabethan England*, London: Sphere 1973, p. 158.
16. Nicholas P. Canny, 'The ideology of English colonisation from Ireland to America', *William and Mary Quarterly*, vol. 30, 1973, p. 581.
17. John Ranelagh, *Ireland*, London: Collins 1981, p. 86.
18. Nicholas P. Canny, *op. cit.*, p. 582.
19. *Ibid.*, p. 576.
20. Ned Lebow, 1973, *op.cit.*, pp. 13-14.
21. *Ibid.*, p. 8.
22. *Ibid.*, p. 9.
23. Kenneth Neill, *The Irish People*, p. 61.
24. Ned Lebow, *op. cit.*, p. 15.
25. *Ibid.*, p. 16.
26. Kenneth Neill, *The Irish People*, p. 61.
27. Mary Campbell, *Paddy in his wellies*, radio documentary, BBC Radio 4, 29 December 1983.
28. Kenneth Neill, *op. cit.*, p. 68.
29. Nicholas P. Canny, *op. cit.*, p. 593.
30. *Ibid.*, p. 596.
31. Folarin Shyllon, *Black People in Britain 1555-1833*, Oxford University Press 1977, p. 93.
32. John Ranelagh, *Ireland*, London: Collins 1981, p. 45.
33. ed. Seán Ó Tuama, *An Duanaire, 1600-1900: Poems of the Dispossessed*, Ireland: The Dolmen Press, 1981, pp. 85-7.
34. Ned Lebow, 'British historians and Irish history', *Eire-Ireland*, vol. VIII no. 4, Winter 1973, pp. 20-1.
35. Christopher Hill, *God's Englishman Oliver Cromwell and the English Revolution*, London: Weidenfeld and Nicholson 1970, p. 118.
36. *Ibid.*, title page.
37. *Ibid.*, p. 113.
38. Paul Johnson, *Ireland*, London: Granada 1981, p. 50.
39. ed. Taylor Downing, *The Troubles*, London: Thames/MacDonald Futura 1980, p. 13; John Ranelagh, *op. cit.*, p. 106.
40. Christopher Hill, *The World Turned Upside Down*, Penguin 1975, p. 122; A.L. Morton, *A People's History of England*, Berlin: Seven Seas 1965, p. 257.
41. Christopher Hill, 1975, *op. cit.*, pp. 336-7.
42. H.N. Brailsford, *The Levellers and English Revolution*, Nottingham: Spokesman Books 1976, pp. 501-2.
43. Christopher Hill, 1975, *op. cit.*, p. 337.
44. ed. Seán Ó Tuama, *op. cit.*, pp. 107-9.
45. *A Collection of Some of the Massacres Committed on the Irish*, London, 1660
46. Quoted in Peter Berresford Ellis, *To Hell or Connaught*, London: Hamish Hamilton 1975, p. 149.
47. See Alvin M. Josefhy Jnr., *The Indian Heritage of America*. USA: Alfred Knopf 1968.
48. *A chorographical description of West H-iarr Connaught*, 1684, quoted in Peter Berresford Ellis, 1975, *op. cit.*
49. Ned Lebow, 'British historians and Irish history', *Eire-Ireland*, vol. VIII no. 4, Winter 1973, p. 18.
50. *Ibid.*, p. 22.
51. John Ranelagh, *Ireland*, London: Collins 1981, p. 130; see also different translation in ed. Seán Ó Tuama, *op. cit.*, p. 151.

52. John Ranelagh, *op. cit.*, p. 126.
53. J.H. Plumb, *England in the Eighteenth Century (1714-1815)*, Penguin 1950, 1969, p. 180.
54. *A Modest Proposal*, reproduced in ed. John Hayward, *Selected Prose Works of Jonathan Swift*, London: The Cresset Press MCMXLIX.
55. Mary Campbell, 'Paddiana: an analysis of anti-Irish "jokes"', *Irish Democrat*, July 1977.
56. Richard Lovell Edgeworth and Maria Edgeworth, *Essay on Irish Bulls*, London, 4th edition 1815, p.41.
57. Ned Lebow, *op. cit.*, p. 19.
58. *Ibid.*, pp. 18-19.
59. *Ibid.*, p. 59.
60. *Ibid.*, p. 27.
61. *Ibid.*, p. 29.
62. Mary Campbell, *Paddy in his wellies*, radio documentary, BBC Radio 4, 29 December 1983.
63. *Ibid.*.
64. J.H. Plumb, *England in the Eighteenth Century (1714-1815)*, Penguin 1950, 1969, p. 33.
65. *Ibid.*, p. 158.
66. *A True-born Englishman*, reproduced in ed. James T. Boulton, *Selected Writings of Daniel Defoe*, Cambridge University Press 1975.
67. See Eric Williams, *From Columbus to Castro*, London: Andre Deutsch 1970; Eric Williams, *Capitalism and Slavery*, London: Andre Deutsch 1964; *Roots of Racism* and *Patterns of Racism*, London: Institute of Race Relations 1982.
68. Quoted in *The British Empire*, vol. 1, London: Orbis 1979, pp. 98-9; see also Peter Fryer, *Staying Power: The History of Black People in Britain*, London: Pluto Press 1984, pp. 102-12.
69. Peter Fryer, *op. cit.*, p. 152.
70. *Ibid.*, p. 99.
71. Folarin Shyllon, *Black People in Britain 1555-1833*, Oxford University Press 1977, p. 199.
72. Ned Lebow, 'British historians and Irish history', *Eire-Ireland*, vol. VIII, no. 4, Winter 1973, p. 11.
73. J.H. Plumb, *op. cit.*, p. 171.
74. *Ibid.*, p. 178.
75. Eric Williams, *British Historians and the West Indies*, London: Andre Deutsch 1966, pp. 49, 52.
76. From 'Locksley Hall', *The Works of Alfred Lord Tennyson*, London Macmillan, 1892.
77. Eric Williams, 1966, *op. cit.*, p. 81.

78. Flann Campbell, *The Orange Card: racism, religion and politics in Northern Ireland*, London: Connolly Publications 1979, p. 12.
79. Peter Berresford Ellis, *A History of the Irish Working Class*, London: Gollancz 1972, p. 112.
80. Richard Ned Lebow, *White Britain and Black Ireland: the influence of stereotypes on colonial policy*, Philadelphia USA: Institute for the Study of Human Issues 1976, p. 44.
81. *Ibid.*, p. 62.
82. *Ibid.*, p. 40.
83. *Ibid.*, p. 39.
84. *Ibid.*, p. 43.
85. John Darby, *Dressed to Kill: cartoonists and the Northern Ireland conflict*, Belfast: Appletree Press 1983, p. 39.
86. Richard Ned Lebow, 1976, *op. cit.*, p. 46.
87. *Ibid.*.
88. *Ibid.*, p. 48.
89. *Ibid.*, p. 53.
90. *Ibid.*, p. 57.
91. *Ibid.*, p. 67.
92. *Ibid.*
93. L.P. Curtis Jr., *Anglo-Saxons and Celts: A study of anti-Irish prejudice in Victorian England*, USA: Conference on British Studies, University of Bridgeport, Connecticut, 1968, p. 70.
94. *Ibid.*, p. 51.
95. *Ibid.*, p. 61; p. 134, n. 40.
96. Eric Williams, *British Historians and the West Indies*, London: Andre Deutsch 1966, pp. 53-4.
97. L.P. Curtis Jr., 1968, *op. cit.*, pp. 102-3.
98. *Ibid.*, p. 63.
99. *Ibid.*, p. 86; see also Flann Campbell, *op. cit.*, p. 13.
100. Eric Williams, 1966, *op. cit.*, p. 177.
101. L.P. Curtis Jr., 1968, *op. cit.*, p. 46.
102. Quoted in *Sinn Fein Weekly*, 26 September 1914.
103. L.P. Curtis Jr., 1968, *op. cit.*, p. 81.
104. *Ibid.*, p. 84.
105. Lewis P. Curtis Jr., *Apes and Angels: The Irishman in Victorian Caricature*, Newton Abbot: David and Charles 1971, p. 100.
106. Richard Ned Lebow, *White Britain and Black Ireland: the influence of stereotypes on colonial policy*, Philadelphia USA: Institute for the Study of Human Issues 1976, p. 83.
107. Quoted in Daniel Evans, *The Life and Work of William Williams*, Llandysul, 1940, p. 85.
108. Mary Campbell, *Paddy in his wellies*,

'The Irish Frankenstein' by Meadows, from Punch in 1843

THE IRISH FRANKENSTEIN.

W w ⁄⁄ ⁄⁄

W is the Word
Of an Englishman true
When given, it means
What he says, he will do
W..W.

radio documentary, BBC Radio 4, 29 December 1983.

109. Bernard Porter, *The Lion's Share: A short history of British imperialism 1850-1970*, London: Longman 1975, p. 132. The other quotations in this section are also taken from Porter's book, pp. 119, 136, 184, 126, 114.

110. *Ibid.*, p. 135.

111. *Ibid.*, p. 181.

112. L.P. Curtis Jr., *Anglo-Saxons and Celts: A study of anti-Irish prejudice in Victorian England*, USA: Conference on British Studies, University of Bridgeport, Connecticut, 1968, p. 53.

113. Lord Birkenhead, *Rudyard Kipling*, London: W.H. Allen, 1980, pp. 287, 300.

114. Richard Ned Lebow, 1976, *op. cit.*, p. 60.

115. Flann Campbell, *The Orange Card: racism, religion and politics in Northern Ireland*, London: Connolly Publications 1979, p. 15.

116. Michael Farrell, *Northern Ireland: The Orange State*, London: Pluto Press 1980, p. 90.

117. Geoffrey Bell, *The Protestants of Ulster*, London: Pluto Press 1976, p. 117.

118. *Ibid.*, p. 42.

119. Reproduced in *World in Action Special: Here We Stand*, Channel 4, 9 February 1984.

120. *Ibid.*

121. Brian Parsons, *Mad Micks and Englishmen: A look at anti-Irish racism*, BA Sociology dissertation, 1983, p. 121.

122. *Irish News*, 12 June 1984; see also *Irish Times*, 30 May 1984.

123. For the songs quoted here, see Geoffrey Bell, 1976, *op. cit.*

124. *Searchlight*, May 1984.

125. *Irish Times*, 30 April 1984.

126. Benedict Anderson, *Imagined Communities: Reflections on the origin and spread of nationalism*, London: Verso/NLB 1983, p. 129.

127. *Catholic Herald*, 14 July 1923.

128. M. Ghodsian and J. Essen, 'The children of immigrants: social and home circumstances', *New Community*, Winter 1980, pp. 195-205.

129. A.L. Rowse, *The Expansion of Elizabethan England*, London: Sphere 1973, p. 139; previous quotations from pp. 114, 121, 131.

130. Josephine Tey, *The Franchise Affair*, Penguin 1948, 1961, p. 179.

131. Robert Taylor, 'Images of the Irish', *New Society*, 28 November 1974.

132. James Callaghan, *A House Divided*, 1973.

133. John Darby, *Dressed to Kill: cartoonists and the Northern Ireland conflict*, Belfast: Appletree Press 1983, p. 53.

134. *Sunday Times*, 28 August 1983.

135. *New Standard*, 19 November 1980.

136. *Sunday Times*, 13 March 1977.

137. Mary Hickman, 'The Problematic Irish': An analysis of the presentation of Britain's relationship to Ireland in school texts, M Sc Sociology dissertation, London: Polytechnic of the South Bank, 1980; see also *Troops Out*, vol. 6 no. 1, October 1982, p. 5.

138. G.W.O. Windward, *Divided Island* Heineman 1976.

139. *Sunday Telegraph*, 3 May 1981.

140. *Times*, 23 September 1977.

141. *Times*, 10 December 1982.

142. Quoted in *Irish Post*, 29 May 1982.

143. *Sunday Express*, 29 January 1984.

144. *Sunday Times Magazine*, 18 December 1983.

145. *Irish Times*, 10 September 1983.

146. Bernard Shaw, *The Matter with Ireland*, London: Hart-Davis 1962, p. 34.

147. Seamus Heaney, *An Open Letter*, Derry: Field Day 1983.

148. *Irish Times*, 29 May 1982.

149. *Daily Express*, 18 October 1971; *Sunday Times*, 24 October 1971.

150. *Irish Post*, 4 December 1982; also see *Standard*, 24 November 1982; *Irish Post*, 26 February 1983; *Guardian*, 8 April 1983.

151. Quoted in *Irish Times*, 21 April 1983.

152. Edmund Leach, 'The official Irish jokesters', *New Society*, 20/27 December 1979.

153. See *Guardian*, 8 June 1984; for subsequent examples in this section see *Hibernia*, 8 October 1976; *Irish Post*, 9 October 1982; *Irish Post*, 27 November 1982; *Irish Post*, 3 July 1982.

154. Edmund Leach, *op. cit.*

155. *Irish Times*, 20 March 1979.

156. Quoted in *Irish Times*, 30 July 1982

157. *Sun*, 23 December 1982; see also *Islington Gazette*, 28 October 1983.

158. *Standard*, 3 November 1983; *Daily Star*, *Sun*, *Daily Mirror*, 4 November 1983; *Sunday People*, 6 November 1983.

159. Richard Lovell Edgeworth and Maria Edgeworth, *Essay on Irish Bulls*, London, 4th edition 1815, p. 8; subsequent quotations pp. 18, 71-2.

THERE WERE THESE THICK PADDIES........

FURTHER READING

Geoffrey Bell, *The Protestants of Ulster*, London: Pluto Press 1976.

Peter Berresford Ellis, *A History of the Irish Working Class*, London: Gollancz 1972, revised edition forthcoming from Pluto Press.

Flann Campbell, *The Orange Card: Racism, Religion and Politics in Northern Ireland*, London: Connolly Publications 1979.

Lewis P. Curtis Jr., *Apes and Angels: The Irishman in Victorian Caricature*, Newton Abbot: David & Charles 1971.

Liz Curtis, *Ireland: The Propaganda War*, London: Pluto Press 1984

John Darby, *Dressed to Kill: Cartoonists and the Northern Ireland Conflict*, Belfast: Appletree Press 1983.

Michael Farrell, *Northern Ireland: The Orange State*, London: Pluto Press 1980.

Peter Fryer, *Staying Power: The History of Black People in Britain*, London: Pluto Press 1984.

A. L. Morton, *A People's History of England*, London: Gollancz 1938, Berlin: Seven Seas 1974.

Séan Ó Tuama (editor), *An Duanaire, 1600-1900: Poems of the Dispossessed*, Ireland: The Dolmen Press 1981.

Roots of Racism and *Patterns of Racism*, London: Institute of Race Relations 1982.

Eric Williams, *British Historians and the West Indies*, London: André Deutsch 1966.

Eric Williams, *From Columbus to Castro*, London: André Deutsch 1970.

Right: detail from the Book of Kells

SÁSTA

Nothing But The Same Old Story was first published by Information on Ireland in 1984 with support from the then Greater London Council, as part of its anti-racism campaign. The book was very well received and rapidly became a classic.

It is now reprinted by Sásta, a voluntary publishing group based in Belfast. If you would like details of our other publications, send a stamp addressed envelope to: Sásta, The Ashton Centre, 5 Churchill Street, Belfast BT15 2BP.

If you enjoyed this book, you may also enjoy

THE CAUSE OF IRELAND:
From the United Irishmen to Partition
by Liz Curtis

The Cause of Ireland tells the story of the background to partition in a clear and vivid way. It was nominated for an Irish Times Literature Prize.

'It deserves to be read widely, especially by young people.' *The Irish Times*

'A splendid book.' *The Irish Post*

The Cause of Ireland is available from: Beyond the Pale Publications, PO Box 337, Belfast BT9 7BT. Price £12.95 (add £1.25 p&p). ISBN 0 9514229 6 0.